HOLE IN THE ~~WIND~~
F 474 K

DATE DUE

AP 19 '96			

Books by Richard Rhodes

NONFICTION

FARM

THE MAKING OF THE ATOMIC BOMB

LOOKING FOR AMERICA

THE INLAND GROUND

FICTION

SONS OF EARTH

THE LAST SAFARI

HOLY SECRETS

THE UNGODLY

A HOLE IN THE WORLD

An American Boyhood

RICHARD RHODES

A TOUCHSTONE BOOK
Published by Simon & Schuster
New York London Toronto Sydney Tokyo Singapore

TOUCHSTONE
Simon & Schuster Building
Rockefeller Center
1230 Avenue of the Americas
New York, New York 10020

1 3 5 7 9 10 8 6 4 2

1 3 5 7 9 10 8 6 4 2 (Pbk)

Library of Congress Cataloging in Publication Data

Rhodes, Richard.
A hole in the world : an American boyhood / Richard Rhodes.
p.   cm.
1. Rhodes, Richard—Childhood and youth.   2. Kansas City (Mo.)—
Biography.   3. Kansas City (Mo.)—Social life and customs.
I. Title.
F474.K253R56   1990
977.8'411043'092—dc20
[B]   90-9949
                        CIP

ISBN: 0-671-69066-3
ISBN: 0-671-74725-8 (pbk)

For Stanley and Richard

Family Album

page 16   Georgia Saphronia Collier Rhodes, c. 1930.

page 19   Georgie as a girl.

page 24   Stanley Rhodes in Des Moines at three.

page 29   ABOVE: Richard, Arthur and Stanley Rhodes on the Gernhardt front porch. BELOW: Stanley Rhodes, unidentified neighbor and Richard Rhodes in the Gernhardt side yard.

page 36   Stanley, Mack and Richard Rhodes on the Gernhardt front steps, c. 1940.

page 45   Arthur and Richard Rhodes.

page 50   Richard and Stanley Rhodes. Stan: "Dad socked on us to get us to straighten up so they could take the picture. You can see the tears in our eyes."

page 56   Arthur Rhodes (in California?) as a young man.

page 126 Stanley, Arthur and Richard Rhodes under stepmother's shadow, summer 1949.

page 127 Richard and Stanley Rhodes and "James Schonmeier," healthy, in Utica, summer 1947.

page 184 The Andrew Drumm Institute, Independence, Missouri.

page 187   George C. Berkemeier and Harry Nelson.

page 204   Richard Rhodes (second from left), c. 1950.

page 250   Stanley Rhodes (third from left) at his Drumm graduation, May 1954.

page 263   Richard Rhodes (fourth from left) at his Drumm graduation, May 1955.

page 270   Richard Rhodes as a Yale senior, 1959.

The things of a man for which we visit him were done in the dark and cold.

—RALPH WALDO EMERSON

1

Metamorphoses

We weave our memories into narrative, from which we construct our identities.

—LEONARD SHENGOLD
Soul Murder

1

WHEN I WAS thirteen months old, my mother killed herself. So I eventually learned, as I learned her maiden name, Georgia Saphronia Collier, and where she was born, Sulphur Springs, Arkansas, and how old she was when she ended her life, twenty-nine. (And good lord, writing these words now, all these years afterward, for the first time in memory my eyes have filled with tears of mourning for her. What impenetrable vessel preserved them?) I didn't know my mother, except as infants know. At the beginning of my life the world acquired a hole. That's what I knew, that there was a hole in the world. For me there still is. It's a singularity. In and out of a hole like that, anything goes.

Since I started childhood as a half-orphan, and along the way endured a wicked stepmother, huckleberry wanderings, years of orphanage life and preparations for a trip to Mars, I want to emphasize here, at the outset, that I understand that the world is full of terrible suffering, compared to which the small inconveniences of my childhood are as a drop of rain in the sea. My older brother Stan, Stanley, suffered more, protecting me. I reconstruct my childhood because that's the spring that seems to be flowing at the moment, something else gushing from the hole, which in one of its manifestations is a fountain.

I was saving the story for fiction, a red giant set somewhere near the end of the world, something Wagnerian. I told a friend, Tracy Kidder, about my childhood and he said, "You should write it just like that, just the way you told it to me," and I said, "No, I'm saving it, I want to orchestrate it, I have a three-volume novel in mind to build on it, a long prose fiction sweeping from the inferno to paradise, I've been making notes toward it for ten years now." I haven't given up on that project either but in the meantime here I am, *a cappella*, I can do no other. The truth is, I finally got your attention.

My mother shot herself in the bathroom of the little white bungalow house where we lived, on Alden Street in Kansas City, Kansas, on Monday morning, July 25, 1938, the nadir year of the Great Depression. She slipped the stick that weighted the linen bathroom window shade from its slot, sat on the toilet, put her mouth around the muzzle of a 12-gauge shotgun and used the stick to push the trigger. I was in my crib. I would have heard the explosion. Stanley was up and playing. He found the oceanic body draining its sea of blood.

I've come to think of my mother as a Depression casualty. Not all the suicides of those days jumped from the windows of Wall Street. One of my mother's two older sisters, my Aunt Espy, speculates that Georgie was pregnant again. She had a ten-year-old, a two-year-old and a one-year-old in her care the day she died. Some in the family thought my father murdered her. He was hard on her, Espy says, he didn't give her enough money for groceries, but she doesn't believe he murdered her. According to my birth certificate, my father, Arthur Rhodes, was a boilermaker for the Missouri Pacific railroad with thirteen years' seniority that year. Stanley ran down a newspaper story at the library when he was a junior in high school, an inch or two of text buried back among the obituaries, no big deal, that placed Dad at work the day our mother died. Espy had lived five houses away on Alden, a comfort to Georgie. "I sewed every stitch of clothes you kids had," Espy told me. But she and Glen, her husband, had recently moved out to Grandview, Missouri, to my grandparents' farm. "She was unhappy to see me go. She really hated it because we moved away."

All of that and more, more than she could bear. I came across Dad's explanation while writing this book, fifty years after the fact. A social worker interviewed him when I was twelve. I only recently saw the report. "The father in telling about the mother," the social worker writes, "tells that he had in a kidding way told her he was going out to the State of Washington and find a blonde. The mother left a note stating that this may not be true but she believed he did mean it." They fought during the weekend. He threatened to leave her. She decided to leave him first, Monday morning, after he went to work. Why was there a shotgun in the house?

I have a photograph of my mother when she was a child, seven or eight years old. Itinerant photographers with darkrooms mounted on horse-drawn wagons took such photographs; you can see where Walker Evans found his style. She's standing in front of a whitewashed wall in a white lace dress. Her hair's parted in the middle, pulled back, held with a wide, dark bow. She's posing so seriously she's almost sad. "She had skin just as white as milk," Espy says. "She had strawberry-blond hair. She had freckles. She had green eyes just like Stan. Stan reminds me of her." She looks like Stan in the photograph, freckles on her forehead and across her nose. She looks like me, a high, wide forehead and a slightly cleft chin, except that I'm ruddy and have red hair. She's wearing cotton stockings and heavy lace-

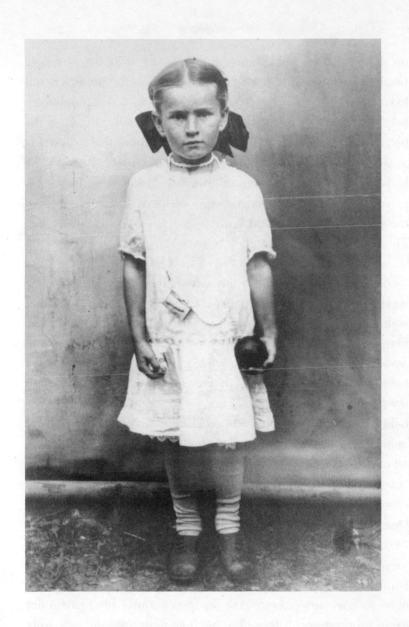

up shoes. A little purse cants at her waist from a long swing of beads looped around her neck like a choker. She holds a handkerchief wadded in her right hand and a dark ball cupped in her left. Espy gave me the photograph. I asked her about the ball. "Oh, that's an orange," she said. "Your mother was sickly as a child. Mother took her to the doctor in town. He said she had rickets. He prescribed an orange a day. Oranges were expensive." That was in the Ozarks, northern Arkansas, around the end of the First World War. "Georgie got to eat the orange. The rest of us ate the peel."

Pat, my other aunt, and Espy and Georgie were my Grandma Collier's second family. Her first husband, whose name was Shields, had picked up and walked off one day and left her with two boys to raise, my uncles Sam and Ray. They got to be big, florid men who liked to jig our heads, Stanley's and mine, with a knuckle; I thought they were Dad's brothers until Espy set me straight. Grandpa Collier was a good man. He married my grandmother and took on her boys. "Mother worked in the field when her babies was little," Espy says. "She'd put her babies in a box and put the box under a bush to keep the sun off of it. She'd hoe the corn. She knew how to make hominy out of wood ashes. We had sorghum molasses in big kegs. We made sauerkraut." After the three girls, two more boys came along. One died of whooping cough. The other was scalded to death. "You boiled your clothes in those days. Somehow that little boy turned over that tub of clothes Mother had set out on the front porch. I don't know, maybe he was playing with that stick she used to stir the clothes." He screamed and Grandma Collier came running out to find him tangled. Espy told me that story just the other day. I'd never heard it before. I'd never seen the tintypes she keeps of our forebears. I have as much family as anyone else after all. I thought I was a mutation, a new line, *sui generis* or at least *non sequitur*.

The bottom dropped out of hog farming when Espy was seventeen, in 1921. "The farm done petered out," she says. The Colliers retreated to South Dakota, where my Grandpa Collier's brother lived. Espy met Glen in the wheat fields of South Dakota the next summer when she was working as a cook for the threshing crews. They courted through the summer and then married. Their marriage lasted until Glen's death from cancer sixty-six years later. At the end he'd only let Espy take care of him. The nurses kidded her. "He thinks you're perfect," they said.

From South Dakota the Colliers returned southward to Grandview, which was a small town then, out in the country a bus ride below Kansas City on the Missouri side of the state line (there are two Kansas Cities, one in Kansas, one in Missouri, divided by the Kaw and Missouri rivers and the state line). I have photographs of my mother as a young woman that Espy gave me. She's slim, pretty, clear eyes, clear skin, carefully dressed. Dressed in a dark sheath of calf-length silk, her hair cut in a page-boy cap, to go out dancing with a dapper, bow-tied man. Kneeling a few years later in a light cotton dress with my dad beside a porch grown up with hollyhocks, my brother Mack, her firstborn, a three-year-old in knee pants between them. A stranger. I don't know her. I know a grave. If she hadn't killed herself she'd probably still be alive. Her older sisters are. Fifty years of her. I can't imagine. I'm sorry for her pain, but what pain she inflicted on us all with her selfish suicide.

Dad was a boilermaker's helper, not a boilermaker. I don't know that he ever got to be a boilermaker. He was a boilermaker's helper until diesel engines replaced steam engines after the Second World War. He went away for training then in diesel mechanics. He was gone so long the hole enlarged. I began to be afraid that he was never coming back.

He worked in a vast roundhouse in the Missouri River bottoms below the river bluffs in northeastern Kansas City, down a long, rickety descent of wooden steps from the end of the trolley car line. He took Stanley and me there once to show us. We rode a little trolley he called the Dinky. The track ended in a barricade. The Dinky was made of wood and had padded wicker seats. The conductor drove it standing up. He turned it around by detaching the operating handle, cranking the sign and walking from one end of the car to the other flipping the wicker seat backs. In the rear he attached the operating handle and cranked the other sign. That made the rear the front. Each end had a brake pedal. When the conductor was ready to go he clanged the bell, wound up the singing electric motors and clicked away.

The stairs and the walk north toward the river through blocks of warehouses made my legs tired. I held Dad's hand. The roundhouse filled the world. Across the threshold of its continental door we entered a darkness of brick and soot-blackened windows, a cavern of hammers and forges, a huge smithy. Steam locomotives long and looming as ocean liners could be clocked around on track sections within its vastness and repaired. The forges glowed like campfires. The hammer faces rang like bells and threw firefalls of iron sparks. Sulfur and iron gritted the air, cinders of coal smoke scratched my eyes, but the smell was the smell of fireworks and the Fourth of July, the day I was born, the day everyone in America celebrated.

When I remember my father, I remember first of all that he was missing the first two joints of the little finger of his left hand. He'd thump us on the head with that blunt stub when we provoked him. A drop hammer had claimed the finger, a machine for forging rivets and shaping plates. He led the way among the locomotive docks to approach the very hammer, its sand-cast and blackened bulk towering up into the gloom, its flat, polished forge faces shining before us. "I felt something wet in my glove," Dad told us. "I pulled off the glove and the finger came off with it." The great hammer secmed a sucking maw then and I shied. I could hardly breathe until we left the building. The sunlight from the river washed the dread away. I thought I might have dreamed the roundhouse. The scale of the place, steam engines and hammers tall as obelisks and fiery furnaces, shadows flickering gigantic across the black floors, filled me with glory. My father moved at ease in those surroundings. No wonder his shoulders and his arms bulged with muscle. He could stand us up one on each hand like dolls.

IIe was forty-four the year my mother died. "You were left with me," he wrote me once defensively, "and i did the best i could." He had three young sons. People offered to adopt us, Espy says, especially the baby, me. We were a popular adoption item, English country stock on both sides, Collier and Rhodes, a grandmother named Shanks. In another era our mother's suicide might have advertised a taint of madness in the blood. The Depression allayed that bigotry. Dad wouldn't hear of adoption. He'd lost his wife. He wasn't giving up his sons.

He parted us out for a while. Day care hadn't been invented yet, not for boilermakers' helpers. Dad had to find a boardinghouse willing to take on at least an infant and a two-year-old. Tall order. Espy and Glen kept me for three months. Stanley went to Des Moines with Uncle Ray. He remembers a cousin, Jewel. "The cousin became my mother and looked after me and

To Daddy
from
Stanley
age 3 yr. 6 mo.

loved me and so forth." His earliest memory is getting into a car at a farmhouse where everyone is solemn, sitting on a woman's lap and crying all the way to Iowa. "They lived right off the highway. They took me into a shed and showed me a little green tricycle. And this cheered me up." Not for long. After Georgie's suicide, the social worker learned from Dad twelve years later, "boy would hang his head and not talk to anyone. When he visited his uncle they took him to a doctor. The doctor said this would be impressed on his mind for a long time." Uncle Ray applied a sovereign American remedy to Stanley's grief. It's advertised in a photograph mounted in a cardboard frame he sent along to Dad: my brother in pinto chaps, a bandanna around his neck and a cowboy hat on his head, sitting on a pinto pony. At three years and six months his eyes are still sad, but his smile is unobstructed. He's expurgated from memory the death he witnessed and its cause.

Our paternal grandfather, Henry Alford Rhodes, whom I never knew, lived in Washington State with Dad's sister Birdie and her husband. Mack went out to live with them. He disappeared from my life for seven years, appeared for one night and disappeared for seven more. So I remember, but I see a photograph in the sketchy family album I've managed to assemble of Stanley and me with Mack when I was three or four. It seems he came to visit. I didn't know him as a child. The brother of my childhood was Stanley, my guardian angel, who saved my life.

2

AFTER MY MOTHER'S DEATH, as if we needed ballast, we moved to a neighborhood on the east side of Kansas City, Missouri, massive with rough limestone. Knobby porches extended like drawbridges from rocky fortresses with windows set deep in their walls. Limestone shoring capped with jagged crenellations and softened with cascades of golden-orange tiger lilies held yards in place beside street cuts. Limestone underlay all that region of western Missouri and eastern Kansas; in the Mississippian era, two hundred million years past, it had thickened with echinoderms and foraminifera under a shallow sea. I was small enough to notice ants entering the world through holes in the joints of the concrete sidewalks. I didn't miss the chalky crinoid segments and fragments of trilobites that conglomerated to limestone. What had been living water now was rock, porch columns and the walls of houses, rock still cool on summer mornings as water under my hand. The world was enormous and enormously minute and I saw it all unblurred. Death had come and gone, darkness spilling into the world and a life ablated before I had capacity to mourn it. Time hadn't started yet for me.

The house we moved to was limestone up to the second

floor. A German family, the Gernhardts, took us in. Mrs. Gernhardt wore an apron and braided her hair. "I can remember
winter days when we had potato soup with butter floating on
top," says Stan. "Lots of pepper and stuff." I remember baked
apples with nutmeg sauce, French toast, bottles of milk with
cream in the neck, pfeffernüsse. "We had all kinds of goodies.
She'd bake things that were just absolutely marvelous." Mr.
Gernhardt was wiry and dark. He sang "Mademoiselle from
Armentières" and some of the verses were naughty. *The third
marine he ate a bean and blew a hole in a submarine, hinky
dinky parlez-vous.* When they didn't want us to know, they spoke
German. They had three adopted children. Heavy Lois in her
wheelchair held me. I was the baby in the family and I was
Baby in that house. I even called myself Baby, in the third
person; "Baby want a di di dee" meant Baby wanted a drink of
water. Who did Baby love best? Baby loved Lois best. When
Lois wrote a letter, Baby could lick the stamp and carry the
envelope to the mailbox on the corner but Baby was not to cross
the street. Race out the front door, across the porch, down the
concrete steps, across the green lawn past the big elm, along
the sidewalk to the mailbox. From everlasting to everlasting.

The lawn was soft grass and smelled of earth. We tumbled
down the slope to the sidewalk forever. Spinning, spinning
around. Stop and the sky went round. Fall down. Fall down.
How could the sky go round? The earth bucked like a pony.

Dad said I could catch a robin if I put salt on its tail. I
crept ever so carefully with the saltshaker but the robin always
flew away. Stanley said if I didn't cross my fingers when Dad
took our picture the camera would kill me and I'd die. I crossed
my big fingers and my little fingers both but I was afraid—afraid
because if I kept my hands at my sides the way Dad said I
should there wasn't any way to cross my thumbs.

It snowed one day in April on the lilac bushes and the new pale green leaves. I woke to its surprise in the soft morning. I knew something had happened because the birds weren't singing. A voluptuous seething touched the silence. I looked out the window of our room in the southwest corner of the second floor, the room Mrs. Gernhardt thought the best room in the house. Plump white snowflakes drifting down the air plopped on lilac clusters and the black branches of the big elm and heaped together white on the branches or sagged like jelly and dripped. They edged the air with cold and cleaned it; it tickled my nose like soda pop.

Mr. Gernhardt in his undershirt watered the evening lawn. He made a fan of spray with his thumb and we ran through it. Mrs. Gernhardt and Lois sat on the porch in the breeze. When Betsy was home she might join them. Neighbors watered lawns up and down the street. The men greeted each other along the unfenced green sward. Sometimes they talked. Dad smoked a Camel on the porch steps to let his supper settle. His smoke smelled like burning leaves. Dark gathered the light and left voices, a radio playing. Lightning bugs winked. The streetlights came on. People disappeared indoors to listen to *Fibber McGee and Molly*.

My father sat silent beyond the foot of the bed in the dark, his glowing cigarette a point of light reddening and dimming, guiding me past the shoals into sleep. We shared the double bed. Stanley had an army cot in the corner.

The women came out into the front yard on a sunny afternoon to wash their hair. They brought a white worktable, a white kitchen chair, a white enameled basin, a galvanized bucket and a washboard surfaced with wavy zinc. They set the basin on the table, set the washboard in the basin and leaned it against the chair back for a drain. They carried rainwater from the barrel under the downspout at the corner of the garage behind the house. Mrs. Gernhardt let down the mystery of her long brown hair. Betsy spread it out on the washboard. The rainwater pouring was a braid of light. Soapsuds. They rinsed and rinsed. The last rinse was vinegar, pungent in the balmy air. Lois next, awkward in her polio braces, her sister unwinding her braid. They wore light cottons. Drying their hair. "Their Sweetness and unusual Beauty made my Heart to leap," exclaims Thomas Traherne in equal ecstasy; "I knew not that they were Born or should Die."

A ragman clattered up the street. Two dark, bony horses with wild manes pulled his wagon on iron tires. He was dark and bony like his horses. His eyes burned, sweeping across the lawns. The wagon was piled with rags and broken furniture and dirty mattresses, buckets hanging off. He passed through the neighborhoods collecting. Up the hill from Prospect Avenue he came, sweat flecking his horses. I hid behind the elm. What if he stole me? I never made out his cry. I thought he said, "Eat that pint! Eat that pint!" It faded as he passed on east. —Eat that pint. —Eat. —Pint.

Dad said thunder was potato wagons unloading. I could feel God's heavy potato wagons dropping their tailgates up above the clouds, potatoes rumbling out onto the white fleece. Why didn't they fall through like the rain? When Dad slung me over his shoulder and twirled me around he called, "Sack of taters! Sack of taters!" He found potatoes in the dirt when he washed out my ears. He wouldn't show me. He got my nose but he gave it back.

We went to our mother's grave once a year on Memorial Day. It was a long ride on the streetcar, across the state line to

Kansas City, Kansas, north nearly to the river. Jing jing, the conductor gave Dad change from the coin changer on his belt. We had to transfer twice. The conductor punched our transfers with his shiny punch. I wished I had a shiny punch and a coin changer to wear on my belt. We bought flowers at a white house. Our mother was buried on a hillside around a road from the cemetery gates. The granite marker was flush with the ground. There was a vase beside the stone. Dad filled it with water from a tap up the hill and arranged the flowers. —Here Son you put a flower in. Your Dearest Mother lies buried here.

Stanley was looking sad and I tried to look sad too. Dad trimmed the grass around the stone with his pocketknife. I wanted a pocketknife but I was too little. I might cut myself.

—She's at peace now, Dad said after a while. My mother was in the earth. If the stone tipped open like the door in the mailbox could I see her? I didn't know what she looked like. Was she wound with cloth like the Mummy's Curse? The worms crawl in the worms crawl out the worms play pinochle on your snout. What was pinochle? When we left and the trolley crossed over at least halfway home you could be silly again.

The iceman brought ice in his yellow truck. —How much ice today? Fifty pounds of ice? That's a lot of ice! There were blocks of ice draped with burlap in the truck's cool interior. Cold spilled out onto our bare feet like a waterfall when the iceman raised the door. With his ice pick he chipped pieces clear as glass for us to suck. They had chains of bubbles frozen in. Chips were sharp enough to cut your tongue at first and then you smoothed them. You could drill a hole with nothing harder than your tongue and stick the tip through. The iceman split a hundred-pound block in half with his ice pick, split one of the halves into two cakes, caught them hanging in tongs and hauled

them around to the kitchen, his arms bulging. When he swung
the cakes up into the icebox and released them his tongs clanged.
—Hot day, ma'am. Yes, ma'am, it sure is.

Down in the basement Mrs. Gernhardt put bluing into the
rinse water of the washing machine. She ran the glistening
clothes through the wringer one by one. They stuck out from
the rollers like the tongues of heathen idols, flattened and matte,
blue water draining back. She carried them up the stairs through
the storm-cellar door into the sun of the yard and hung them
on the lines to dry. We coveted her clothespins. We colored
one kind with crayons to make skinny people with pill heads.
The other kind, spring-loaded clamps, we hung from our ear-
lobes or dangled from our lower lips like Ubangis. Mrs. Gernhardt doled them out as frugally as she doled out summer
Fudgsicles. The dry clothes we helped her gather smelled as if
the sun had toasted them.

In the hottest part of summer Paul Gernhardt had to go for
extra ice, west on Thirty-fifth Street and across Prospect Avenue
hauling a red wagon. Paul was in high school. Sometimes Stanley
and I went with him and on the way down I got to ride. From
the house we crossed South Benton Street, Chestnut, Montgall
and then Prospect. I'd never been so far without a grown-up,
out of sight of home, different houses and trees and dogs, women
standing behind screen doors watching, taking us into their
minds and thinking about us, down the long, long hill, then far
in the distance the big familiar snare drum over the door of the
Drumm Cleaners and Launderers on the corner at Prospect. It
was hotter on Prospect. The asphalt stung my summer-hardened
feet. Trucks rumbled by. Big trolley buses boarded grown-ups
who came from somewhere and went somewhere else. Prospect
ran out of sight in either direction to the ends of the profligate

world. I don't remember where we bought the ice. Neighborhood coal companies sold ice in those days from detached icehouses set to the side of their yards like one-room cabins; the blocks stacked inside were shrouded with fog. The cake we brought home rode majestic on its red throne nested in burlap, a glistening iceberg spraying sparks of cold under the summer sun. It was hard hauling the wagon up the hill. —Richard you'd be a help if you'd get behind and push. —Stanley won't let me. Watch out, Stanley. —You watch out you big baby I'll do this.

A hot-tamale man called through the neighborhood with his homemade wooden cart. What were hot tamales? I wondered and wondered. Little boys wouldn't like them.

"We were climbers," Stan says. "We weren't afraid of heights. Dad was petrified. We'd climb the Gernhardts' trees and Dad would say, 'Oh God, get out of there, get out of there.' You know. And finally he'd just let us go. He'd call us monkeys. 'You monkeys.' You know. 'Get out of there, you monkeys.' "

The streetcar company ran a summer trolley with a surrey top. It had wicker seats like the Dinky but it was open to the air. On a hot summer night Dad and Stanley and I rode it down Signboard Hill past Union Station. Returning by the huge station we watched the Sherwin-Williams paint sign rising like a moon above the hill. The sign was a paint bucket of lights tipped over a globe of lights snared like the drum at the Drumm Cleaners. Colored light flowed like paint from the bucket over the globe. Sherwin-Williams Paints Cover the Earth. Before the paint could drip off, the sign blacked out and then the bare grid turned on again and the colored light flowed again like paint. That was painting the town red. —We painted the town red tonight, didn't we, boys. The trolley with the surrey fringe was more fun even than the Ferris wheel at Fairyland Park. Sometimes people rented the surrey trolley for parties and then you could see them go by with the lights on, laughing and drinking beer.

"We also had a rabbit at that location," Stan recalls. "And it died and we were very grief-stricken." Yes. "And Dad was saying things like 'Why are you all upset about a little old rabbit?' " Yes. We buried it and made a cross of twigs and brought carrots and lavender buds of clover to the grave. After a while we forgot. When we remembered, the cross was gone and we couldn't find the grave and we cried again.

I wouldn't drink my milk. No one could make me. —You'll sit there until you do, Dad said. I was in my high chair. Everyone else went outside. Stanley was excused. I could smell the warm milk. It was a flat, creamy circle. If I wiggled my tray the flat would wrinkle and leave a white lip on the side of the glass. There were mirrors in the dining room that reflected other mirrors. I could see myself over and over again getting smaller and smaller until I disappeared. When I moved my head all of us moved our heads smaller and smaller. There were that many smaller and smaller glasses of milk. Dad checked in on me once in a while to see if I'd decided to do as I was told. It got dark. It was past my bedtime. Everyone came back inside. —Fine then we'll put the milk in the icebox and you'll drink it in the morning. See that he drinks his milk will you Mrs. Gernhardt? He has to learn not to waste food. In the morning my milk was cold again. I drank it down. I liked to drink it cold. I didn't like to drink it warm.

In 1940 Mack returned to live with us—the visit I don't remember—before going off to work on a farm south of Kansas City. In one of Espy's photographs he sits on the porch steps at the Gernhardts' with Stanley and me flanking him, a handsome, smiling boy of thirteen. Paul Gernhardt remembers the

visit because Paul got polio that year. In a household of five children—six counting Mack, who took a room on the third floor—two suffered polio and one of the two, Lois, was permanently crippled. Polio was a plague. One day you had a headache and an hour later you were paralyzed. How far the virus crept up your spine determined whether you could walk afterward or even breathe. Parents waited fearfully every summer to see if it would strike. One case turned up and then another. The count began to climb. The city closed the swimming pools and we all stayed home, cooped indoors, shunning other children. Summer seemed like winter then. Movie theaters hurt by the summer quarantine led the way collecting to buy iron lungs, pressure tanks like steam boilers that breathed mechanically for quadriplegic victims who lived inside on pallets, their heads sticking out a gasket into the world. Stan remembers Paul's polio attack. "They took him out in an ambulance one day. Everyone was crying and anxious and they took him out on a stretcher. He came back later and he had one of these horrible braces on his leg, through his shoe. Very thin and weak. And he limped around, and it seemed like he was getting better. You could tell he was getting progressively better." He recovered fully so far as I know. I met him many years later and sailed with him; he was a consulting engineer and a solid family man.

Evenings in late summer the locusts roared in the trees, tough as little bulldogs. They didn't bite or sting, but they were too buzzy to hold cupped in my hands. I collected the crunchy brown shells they left stuck to the trunks of trees when they emerged from the ground and used them for toys, arrayed them in battle, lined them along the sidewalk to engage the ants.

We rode the trolley bus to Montgomery Ward's one day— Monkey Ward's, Dad called it—to buy our winter coats. The boys' department smelled like sizing. In the coat aisle Dad found burgundy corduroy coats with four flap pockets on the front. They belted in front with a corduroy self-belt with D-rings. I didn't know how to loop the belt. Stanley showed me but I still didn't know. It was hard! —Now let's find stocking caps, Dad said. The bins were piled high with clothes. I couldn't see over them. Dad was gone. Stanley was gone. Where were they? Where were they? I ran through the aisles. A man stopped me. Was I lost? My lower lip pouted. I said I was. I wiped my nose on my sleeve. The man took my hand and led me away, across the store to a clear space. He questioned me. —Just stand under this sign, he told me. We'll find your daddy and your brother. Wait right here and I'll have them paged.

The sign was a giant eye. It was wide open. I could feel it up above me staring. All that eye. The man's voice came over a radio saying my name. Richard. A little lost boy. I waited and waited. What if they never came? Then they did. —Where'd you get off to? Dad asked me. He took my hand. —You should stay close by. Stanley made a face. He thought I'd gotten lost on purpose. We bought the corduroy coats and stocking caps and corduroy pants too. We were ready for winter.

The trees lost their leaves. Red leaves, yellow and brown leaves fluttered down the yard and covered the grass. Elm leaves looked like wide, fat feathers, maple leaves like gloves. We raked them to the curb and burned them. If I breathed too much smoke it made me sneeze, but the smoke smelled wonderful. It boiled off the red line of flame so thick at first that I couldn't see through it, brown-white, thinning and paling to blue-white as it swirled up into the air. The fire crackled and raced. When I waved my arm through the smoke it was warm. My arm mixed the swirls and my corduroy sleeve came away smelling smoky.

I fed the fire a leaf at a time, holding each leaf by its stem over a single tongue of flame. First the edges fluttered in the flame. Then a hole popped open where the flame licked from below like the hole that my tongue made in an ice chip. The hole inflamed and opened, eating the leaf away. Before the hole reached the edge, the leaf would crumple and I'd drop it onto the pile and find another. I loved to stare into flame. It was the color of my hair. Already lost from the tree, where did the leaf go? How could smoke and flame carry so much substance away?

After the leaves had burned there was gray ash that the wind took.

It used to snow in Kansas City. The long hill that led down to Prospect was perfect for sledding. We had a wooden sled with red steel runners. We got a good start. Stanley dropped prone and I dropped on top of him, his stocky strong body under me guiding the runners that crunched the ice as we skimmed down the hill. Hauling back up was hard. We went on skimming down and hauling back up again until it got dark. We came in from the cold to the warm house and I fell asleep at supper. When I woke it was morning. The air in the room was cold and I was undressed in my bed. I could hear Dad in the basement stoking the furnace with coal.

Mrs. Gernhardt created a Christmas village in the living room every year, around the Christmas tree, a whole countryside. The land deep with snow was cotton batting. Ponds were mirrors. Cardboard houses had lights in them and their roofs glittered. Horses pulled sleighs among conical pine trees like milk-bottle brushes, molded cows stood in pastures, pigs and 'chickens looked out from barn lots. Crèches of different scales and designs where shepherds kept watch scattered the countryside. Wise men lined up with their gifts and Marys and Josephs knelt over mangers where baby Jesuses lay. The largest crèche was on the mantel, out of reach, but only a miniature picket fence cordoned off the countryside. I had to be told again and again to stay away. I strained to lean far enough across the picket fence to reach the little baby Jesuses in their mangers. I wanted to lift them out, slip them into my pocket, shrink to their size and replace them. I was Baby, baby Jesus, Mary and Joseph's child. Holy infant, holy family, whole, hole. I was drawn to those mangers as I was drawn to flames, entranced. I stared at them for hours.

3

I REMEMBER PEARL HARBOR, December 7, 1941. I was four then, four and a half. Dad was reading the Sunday morning funny papers to us when the news came over the radio. Stanley and I ran shouting from house to house. "The Japs bombed Pearl Harbor! It was on the radio! The Japs bombed Pearl Harbor!" I didn't know what Japs were or where Pearl Harbor was. The words made grown-ups pay attention. People threw open their doors. Strangers called to strangers. Everyone began to talk.

In the years of war the streets became parks where we could play. Buses and streetcars still operated, but automobiles rarely moved us to the curb because gasoline was rationed and no one could get tires. In residential neighborhoods at least, the war turned back the clock.

Bread was delivered in those days just like milk and ice and coal. Manor, the commercial bakery that the Gernhardts used, mothballed its trucks for the duration and reconditioned its old horse-drawn bread wagons. The bread man's horse followed his deliveries from house to house, hauling the wagon up the street on its own when he whistled, a throng of neighborhood kids on the sidewalk pacing it. After the ragman's bony savages I approached it warily. It was dignified, patient and not unfriendly but serious about its work. I ventured to the curb to watch it, breathing its smell of sweat and urine and wondering at its black blinders. I thought they might be meant to shade its eyes. Waiting for the bread man's whistle it seemed to lose itself in thought. It chewed on its metal bit, grinding its teeth and dropping gobbets of greenish drool. Sometimes it shook its great head to scare off flies, jingling its traces. Sometimes, to the collective frenzy of its crowd of admirers, it cocked its tail and dropped baseballs of brown, straw-filled manure onto the street that smelled like oatmeal and steamed grass. When I came to read *Gulliver's Travels* I understood Gulliver's admiration for the Houyhnhnms. They were beings like the bread man's horse, beset by Yahoos. The world was beset by Yahoos in those days, but on this side of the Atlantic at least, the children were spared. The war kept grown-ups too busy and too preoccupied to supervise us closely. We spent the war playing.

We knew the enemy. War propaganda identified him and vilified him, uniting us in hate. We were encouraged to dream of murders that our fathers and brothers actually might commit. The Nazis and the Japs were evil; the British and the Russians were gallant allies. (I was bewildered, after the war, when the Russians in the space of a few months slipped from ally to enemy; I couldn't understand how they went bad so fast.) We went to the movies two or three times a week in those days before television and followed the war in newsreels. Stukas and Japanese Zeros bombed and strafed before our eyes to a narrator's snarl of contempt. B-17s in box formation bristling with ball turrets countered them; Flying Tigers painted with the mouths of sharks spit fire from their wings. Heads like great icons filled the screen: Franklin Delano Roosevelt grinning around his long cigarette holder; Winston Churchill flashing his

42

V-for-victory sign; walrus-mustached Uncle Joe Stalin shrewdly puffing his pipe; buck-toothed, slant-eyed, myopic Hirohito chanting incomprehensible Japanese; Hitler with his ridiculous toothbrush mustache, a lick of hair black down his forehead like an ax gash, stabbing the air with a Nazi *Sieg heil!* salute that we parodied when we played war.

The first movie I remember seeing was *Bambi*. I slouched with Stanley in the front row, Dad avoiding vertigo halfway up the aisle with the other grown-ups, and the animated forest drew me in. Bambi lost his mother and I wept for him. I thought my heart would break. Stan tells me Dad took us to the movies regularly on Saturday afternoons, all the way downtown, favoring Frankenstein and other horrors. The war was dense with death, even in that modest outlier of paradise on Thirty-fifth Street between South Benton and Agnes and Bellefountaine. Gold stars embroidered on fringed black crepe panels like shrunken shades hung in the front windows of houses here and there up and down the street, announcing a lost husband or son or brother. They radiated dread. Discovering that death had visited other families reminded me that death had visited my own. "In a lot of ways," Stan says, "I think Frankenstein, the Wolf Man, Dracula and the comic books we read helped us work out some of this. I'm not sure how much good it did but it gave us a perspective on it." Lurching corpses, noblemen with Central European accents sucking blood, decent fellows turned into hairy, violent brutes under a lunatic moon, were reasonably accurate analogues to the war.

On our way back from the movies we passed a full-grown tree with its trunk twined in a bulbous overhand knot. Someone had knotted it when it was a sapling and it had grown to maturity that way. Stan remembers that Dad always commented on it.

Then we usually stopped for ice cream. "I would always order vanilla ice cream with butterscotch on it," my brother recalls. "You liked, I think it was chocolate." But chocolate was hard to get during the war, like everything else imported, and I can taste the memory of vanilla ice cream sharp with ice crystals and dripped with butterscotch, rich and cold in the heat of Missouri summer; it's mixed up with the taste of snow ice cream Mrs. Gernhardt made for us once after an early autumn storm. Eventually meat and sugar both were rationed. Dad turned over our sheets of ration coupons, stamps bound in little books, to the Gernhardts every week.

But we didn't go with Dad only to movies and ice-cream parlors, Stan says. On some of those Saturday afternoons we detoured to the Folly Theater on Twelfth Street to catch a burlesque show. I wish I remembered those afternoons. In the childhood of my selective recollection my father came home every night directly from work and never went out; he had no erotic life at all. In fact he was dragging us to burlesque shows or, later, dropping us off at movies and slipping away to visit girlfriends on the side. "There was a live, scroungy band that played," Stan recalls, "and a slapstick comic. There was a woman with bubbles and fans who was completely naked on the stage"—could she have been Sally Rand?—"and he was just there with his eyes open, and then he'd kind of look over at us. He had a Saturday disappearance, and that's one reason we went to so many Saturday movies. He had several girlfriends." Normal enough, and Dad was a handsome man—muscular, broad-shouldered, with a strong jaw and thick, wavy hair. I understand why I wouldn't have noticed his comings and goings when I was five, but why did the news still surprise me four decades later? I had a terrible nightmare in early middle age, one of the worst

of my life, in the midst of a long course of healing psychotherapy, after Dad died. He came back to haunt me, a skull clamped to a lab bench that I reached out to touch in love and sorrow that began biting and swallowing my hand, eating its way up my arm like a shark. Treacherous depths. I wanted him too much. In the laboratory of psychotherapy I would learn how hazardous it is to long for an ideal father when your real father fails you.

Mr. Gernhardt went off to work as a foreman on the Al-Can Highway, a gravel road the army was building through British Columbia and the Yukon to Alaska's Dutch Harbor to supply our military operations in the Aleutians against the Japanese. He sent us cards at Christmas—"little funny verses on them," Stan says—and returned in 1943 with stories to tell. Stan braved the Al-Can Highway as a young man, bent on homesteading in Alaska. Mr. Gernhardt's adventure must have reverberated somewhere at the back of his head. He only retreated to the lower forty-eight when he'd patched nine flat tires and exhausted his stake.

Paul Gernhardt adapted to the war by adding unpainted balsa-wood soldiers with articulated joints to his constructions. He built superb model airplanes of balsa wood and tissue paper, all the major fighter aircraft of the war, in a big attic room on the third floor of the house. They were kit airplanes, but hobby kits before injection molding oversimplified them contained only printed plans and special parts such as hooks and canopies and wheels. All the wooden parts—the ribs that formed the wings, the tail structures, the framing for the fuselage—Paul cut by hand and carved and glued himself from sheets of balsa he bought at a neighborhood hobby store. Balsa wood got scarce as the war went on; he salvaged scrap to make his soldiers, several hundred of them eventually, little balsa men no larger than half-used wooden pencils with jointed arms, legs, waists and heads and balsa rifles. I thought they were miraculous.

We lumped Paul's bed and the rag rug on the floor of his room to make a battleground and improvised our own wars under a ceiling hung with resplendent model airplanes dogfighting in the updrafts from the coal furnace three floors below. "Paul made us rubber-band guns that fired strips of old inner tubes," Stan says. He sawed the guns from pine boards. "They had a snap clothespin on the end for a trigger. We'd hide a soldier. His gun and head had to be showing or he couldn't fire. And then I would have to get down on my guy and aim at your guy. Paul always gave us the worst guns. He had the ones with the most zip in them. And the last guy with guys left won, or there was a count or something. We had hours and hours of fun up there."

It seems odd that a boy of high-school age played with toy soldiers. Paul was entertaining us, and maybe he needed play to work out polio or the war. Stan evinces Paul's intellectual range, and his own. "He loved Beethoven. That was my first introduction to Beethoven."

Paul built soapbox cars as well. He carried me as a passenger sometimes on his rides down the long Thirty-fifth Street hill. The hill was a mechanism for storing energy. Soapbox cars and wagons, scooters and sleds and roller skates needed no rationed gasoline to energize its potential, only the muscle power we stoked with tuna casserole and macaroni and cheese and our weekly ration of meat. Paul finished his soapbox cars as meticulously as his model airplanes. He grew up to be an inventor as well as a consulting engineer, called in to solve manufacturing problems when staff engineers found themselves stumped.

We collected tinfoil for the war effort, cooking grease that was supposed to be useful in ammunition-making, newspapers, tin cans. Foil was precious as gold; to help build B-29s to firebomb Japan we stripped Dad's Camel cigarette packs and soaked free the fragile, silvery sheets that backed chewing-gum wrappers. I can remember carrying a ball of foil in my pocket just to have it to admire. Chicle had gone the way of balsa wood and wartime chewing gum was terrible, scarcely dusted with sugar and crumbling after a few minutes of chewing without ever forming a smooth wad. We had better luck chewing street tar or the aromatic resin that oozed from the joints of a neighbor's ornamental pine. I didn't know what bubble gum was until 1946, when our pennies bought pockets full and Stanley won the contest we improvised the day the stuff returned to the stores by chewing twenty-four balls at one time long enough to blow a bubble. His jaw was sore for a week. During the war, songs about separation and loneliness, songs of nostalgia for peacetime, made grown-ups cry. Kids dreamed of assaulting Pacific beaches and taking out Nazi pillboxes and favored patriotic numbers. I still remember the lyrics to "Comin' In on a Wing and a Prayer"—"Though there's one motor gone, / We can still carry on, / Comin' in on a wing and a prayer"—but I'll spare you.

Where in all this Fibber McGee's closet of wartime memory is Lois? I know that her nurturing, along with my father's and aunts' and the Gernhardts', gave me the fundamental security I needed later to survive. Probably I saw less of her. I was outdoors more, and her wheelchair confined her to the house and porch. But it seems to me she withdrew to her room during those years, physically and perhaps psychologically compromised by her paralysis. I remember vividly a day filled with intrigue, Mrs. Gernhardt in and out of Lois's room, muffled

arguments, whisperings among the grown-ups, and then Dad
coming home and an ambulance turning up and Dad and the
ambulance attendants carrying Lois screaming and thrashing
down the stairs, forcing her into a wheelchair, restraining her
arms and legs with leather straps and wheeling her out the door.
I cried for her, seeing her helpless. I didn't know why they were
taking her away. The men forcing her infuriated me. Stanley
had to hold me back. Dad explained to me later that she had
an infected pressure sore on her leg from her braces. She'd been
hiding it. Its smell had finally given it away. She hated the
hospital so much, she'd refused to go voluntarily even if it meant
losing her leg.

Paul wrote me once, out of the blue, after I'd mentioned
my childhood in the introduction to my first book. "Can you
remember Mrs. Gernhardt sitting with you and reading from the
Book of Knowledge?" he asked. "Can you remember her sitting
with you with an old faded globe and pointing out the oceans?
She did that not only with you but with me and with a number
of other young children who lived with us. She had an enormous
supply of love which she freely, if not obviously, gave and she
believed devoutly in education." Which young children? Where
are they now? Why have I forgotten them? Why have time and
pain hidden my past from me? My stepmother's violence, the
barricade of horror she built across my life, drowned my memory
of those years—a dead lake entombing a green valley.

I was Mrs. Gernhardt's star pupil, Paul says; she taught
me to read when I was four going on five, in 1942. I taught my
daughter Kate to read at the same age. Tim, my son, like Stanley,
learned to read in school. It isn't important, we all caught up
soon enough, except that I had the pleasure of seeing Kate make
the connection. I sat her on my lap and read to her, pointing

to the words, asking her to repeat them. She knew the alphabet; she could pick out letters and even spell out words, but she didn't connect them with speech or meaning. "These letters together," I explained again and again, "they're the words you're saying." She'd smile and repeat the words and run her fingers over the letters. And then one day in the middle of a favorite book, probably Dr. Seuss, who ought to have a Nobel, her eyes widened, her face filled with surprise. She'd understood. She read one word and then another, hesitantly at first, looking back and forth between me and the book, asking me for more, seeing them once and committing them to memory, a whole world opening to her comprehension before my eyes. I'll never forget that moment. Mrs. Gernhardt must have known the same pleasure with me.

Stanley took over then. "We learned to read with comic books," he says. "We had the biggest pile of comic books in the whole neighborhood."

"Back when people thought they'd rot your mind," I interject, "and you were using them to teach me to read."

"Of course. And we would spend hours on the floor reading. I would read to you the comic books and I would, you know, go through all the acting movements and everything. And then we would take these comic books in our little red wagon, and we'd roll them down to this little store, and trade them two for one. And we'd come back with a diminished pile, but they would all be more reading material. And we'd go through that pile. We were comic-book crazy. *Plastic Man, Captain Marvel, Crime Busters*. We weren't crazy about *Superman*. Every time we had a dime, and they were all dime comic books, we would read and read and read." The last generation's trash is the next generation's art form—the novel, the motion picture, television yet to come and probably Nintendo after that. You say comic books missed the boat, but what about *Dream and Lie of Franco*?

Once I learned to read I was launched, adrift in dreamtime half the rest of my life. I had already seen past appearances, ants boiling up from the joints in concrete sidewalks, trees tied in knots, limestone compacted of the lives of uncountable billions of individual shells, the burst of saliva in my mouth when Betsy poured vinegar to rinse Lois's hair, the space my mother should have occupied rent like a tear in the fabric of time. Now I saw—because Mrs. Gernhardt started me and my vernacular brother guided me to fluency—that words could boil up worlds that towered overhead like a spring storm, splashed light and shadow the length and width of a city, drove crowds under cover, crashed lightning, uprooted trees, flooded streets, stopped traffic, rumbled away in a passage of cold wind and abruptly dissipated, pure energy, nothing left but clean air and the bright sun shining. That real, that profligate, that leviathan, and all of it open to me without restraint in the pages of books, pouring out into my child's life like Niagara.

4

ALL I HAVE LEFT of my father are these memories and a couple of letters. Stan has five photographs and a narrow pocket notebook from the early 1920s, a bare diary. Mack may have more; I haven't asked him. I wish Dad had left me his pocketknife or his pocket watch. I wish I had his steamer trunk of tools. I only saw him once or twice after I was grown. He gave me an odd legacy on one of those occasions, two small envelopes crammed with fillers clipped from the *Kansas City Star*, brief paragraphs of facts that the newspaper used in Linotype days to fill out columns when stories ran short. He valued facts; his schooling had stopped at the third grade. I was amazed that he'd gone to so much trouble, but I was too callow to understand his enthusiasm for envelopes of magpie clippings, or to see that each clipping preserved in its edges the ephemeral compositions of his hand. After I'd browsed them, angry at their impersonality, I threw them away. I'm sorry now I didn't keep them. They'd give substance to Paul Gernhardt's description of him in the letter Paul wrote me:

> Your dad worked very hard. He was a locomotive repairman and had to go into the still hot boilers to do some of his work. He was

a very powerful man and I recall being amazed at some of his feats of strength. . . . He was rather a quiet man, used to like to read the paper in the evening. I seem to recall him sitting in a woven wicker rocking chair reading the evening paper in your room.

The little that Dad owned he took care of. He had a farmer's respect for tools. He kept his pocketknife sharp. He edged it on an oilstone, careful of the angle. He carried his watch on a leather fob in a watch pocket at his waist and dangled it at my ear when I asked him to let me hear it tick; he wound it formally once a day, springing open the case to check the time and snapping it shut. He always had the correct time; he set his watch by a railroad chronometer at work. He polished his own shoes and taught us to polish ours. One of his belts was carefully stitched together in back where it had broken. Good shoes and belts, he'd tell us, would last fifteen years.

The steamer trunk held his woodworking tools—a common saw and a backsaw, planes, chisels, files, screwdrivers, a brace and an assortment of bits—all carefully oiled. He stored it in the basement. When he unlocked it and lifted the lid it released a musty odor of iron and household oil. Forty years passed before I smelled that distinctive odor again, climbing down a steel ladder into the damp underground target room of one of the old Van de Graaff generators at the Department of Terrestrial Magnetism of the Carnegie Institution of Washington. Niels Bohr, Enrico Fermi, Edward Teller and a gathering of other physicists first saw evidence confirming nuclear fission in that circular room late one Saturday evening in January 1939. I was awed to have descended into so historic a site, really an unsung shrine, but the potent artifact my sense of smell evoked wasn't an iron target piece lined with uranium foil; it was Dad's steamer trunk of woodworking tools.

Dad was forty-nine years old in 1942, when I was five and starting kindergarten. I didn't think of him as old, as Mr. Gernhardt seemed old; he was young physically and his hair hadn't yet grayed. I know very little about the life he lived before he fathered mine. "He almost had to be in the service," Stan says, meaning the First World War.

"Because of his age?"

"Well, yes, that too." My brother frowns. "But I saw a photograph of him in a white navy suit aboard a dreadnought." I remember the same photograph. I mentioned it to Espy. "Anyone can put on a sailor suit," she countered skeptically, and other than the photograph, Dad kept no wartime mementos that I ever saw. Espy said Dad told my mother once, during a fight, that he'd been in prison. If he was out of circulation for a while, I think she meant, it wasn't because he'd gone to sea. Stan doubts that Dad was a felon and so do I, but my evidence is ridiculous: he had a sailor's skill at sewing and kept us in buttons and darned our socks. A sailor would need those skills, but so would a widower. So would a convict, for that matter.

It isn't even clear where Dad was born. My birth certificate and his obituary list his birthplace as Shelbina, Missouri, but he says in one of his letters that he was born in Shelbyville, Shelby County, Missouri, on July 19, 1893. The two towns, in northeastern Missouri not far from Hannibal, are only eight miles apart. Maybe the family farm, if there was a family farm, fell between them.

I asked my brother to send me his old photographs to copy. They were two weeks coming. "It was more difficult than I thought to part with these," he introduced them. I hadn't seen most of the photographs before, photographs of my mother and of Stanley as well as of Dad. Nor Dad's pocket diary, which is black pressed leather, two by four inches hinged vertically,

narrow-ruled loose-leaf pages locked with three small steel rings, with alphabet tabs—really an address book. The diary entries don't help much. The longest covers almost a year:

Aug 22nd 1923
Left Burdick [Kansas]
for K[ansas] C[ity] at 1140
am. Will return
in car Saturday
Aug 25th, 1923.
Miss & Mrs. Edwards
and Eileen came
to the train with me. Left
Strong City [Kansas] at 239 P.M. Left
Burdick for Home
Sept 16th got as
far as Emporia [Kansas]
had to lay over
there until the
19th on account
of rain, returned
to Burdick and
went home again
in Sept about the
20th stopped at
Emporia on way
back to Burdick.
remained there

several days
returned to
Emporia on Mar
25th 1924 going
back to B.[urdick] Sunday
returned to Emp[oria]
on the 27th of April.
Will return to B——
the [blank] of May 1924.
brought the girls down
for a visit.

Maddening. Who are the girls? Dad's sisters? The notebook reveals that on February 18, 1921, with a buddy named Sam Bell, Dad went to Independence, Missouri, and bought a car. What happened to the car? It records the presence of a Miss Billie Rhodes—a cousin?—in Los Angeles in 1920 (I see I'm going through it backward); in one of the photographs that Stan sent me, Dad as a young man wearing a cloth cap, there's a palm tree in the background, so he may have gone to visit her, or one "Chas. Rhodes" of Sacramento. Apparently a previous generation of Rhodeses migrated west before Mack and Stan. When my time came, thinking to fill the hole with culture, I fled east.

"He repaired watches, didn't he?" I ask Stan.

"He was a fix-it man," Stan says. "He was tied in to a little radio shop. He would go there and help the guy and they would work together in the back room. He was always repairing something. And he was good at it." He fixed alarm clocks on a table under a window in one of the furnished rooms we rented, if not at the Gernhardts' then at some other boardinghouse, later. I remember the cacophony of their ticking, each asserting its own time, and I remember the smell of the castor oil he used to lubricate them. I don't think he knew electronics; at the radio shop he probably repaired small appliances.

He repaired us as well. When Stanley and I had chicken pox, two weeks in a darkened room climbing the walls, not even allowed to read, standard treatment in those days because chicken pox was supposed to weaken your eyes, Dad painstakingly dabbed polka dots of Merthiolate wherever we had scratched up infection—everywhere. Merthiolate stung the elbow and hand and knee abrasions I brought to him from playing out of doors, but behind the sting, tickling it, the glass applicator with its smooth knob like a match head was cool.

I gashed my wrist trick-or-treating with Stanley one moonless Halloween, the worst injury of my childhood. I fell on the point of one of a zigzag of bricks that lined a front walk. My brother was furious to have to lead me home and miss out on half an evening's candy, but I didn't know my way and I was bleeding. The gash ran up the middle of my right wrist and separated the skin. A doctor would have sutured it. There was no medical insurance then; people didn't run to emergency rooms easily. Dad cleaned the wound with soap and water, painted it with Merthiolate and approximated it with roller gauze and adhesive tape. It was impressively ghastly for days. I still have the scar.

"You and I got really, really sick one time with some sort of flu or cold or something," says Stan, "and we were singing hymns and carrying on. In those days the doctor came to the house. Here he came with his little black bag and he said, 'Well, these boys are singing, they can't be too sick.' And he put the thermometer in and we were a hundred four or a hundred five and he said, 'We've got to get these temperatures down right now. They're *delirious*, that's why they're singing.' " I remember the figures in the wallpaper dancing. Even without fever I found creatures in the floral wallpaper, especially at the edge of sleep, but that day they were moving.

Stan recalls, and I do not, not the least trace, that Dad spanked us. "Dad was a very vigorous spanker," my brother explains, astonished that I don't remember. "He *spanked*." Although Stan is six feet one and big-boned and his little boy calls him Ironhand for the strength of his grip, there's deference in his voice. He illustrates.

"Okay, we were at the Gernhardts', and I had a pocket watch with a fob—it was just newly purchased. One day I secretly took it all apart, and I couldn't get it back together. I put it back together the best I could. Dad came home and found out that someone had tooken it apart, and he spanked me very hard. And I cried and cried, but I wouldn't admit it. So then he turned to you and spanked you very, very hard. To try to cough up a confession. You looked at me. You knew I'd done it."

"I did?"

"And I knew that I had done it, but neither one of us would confess. So Dad changed his tactics. He not only spanked us, but he said that if one of us didn't confess, we wouldn't get to go see the Frankenstein movie."

I laugh.

"So you confessed."

I'm incredulous. "I confessed that I did it?" For a Frankenstein movie? What happened to my principles?

"You confessed that you did it. So then he gave you a

proper scolding and we went to see the Frankenstein movie."

I'm more incredulous. "And you let this happen?" It's a question, not an accusation.

"And I let this happen, and I was so ashamed of it, for a long, long time."

Stan has another illustration that skews to a different point. "I became very good at jigsaw puzzles. Dad spanked me real hard for something once and then he wanted me to work on a puzzle. I wouldn't. I stopped working on puzzles from then on. I would never touch another puzzle, and it was mainly because I was mad at him. He almost begged me to work on puzzles. And I thought, Well, this is the first time I felt any control over my father. I was amazed that he'd almost begged me. I thought, Gee. You know." Paul Gernhardt wrote me of Stan, Stanley: "I remember him as a small child with a will of iron." He'd need it.

I know why I don't remember the spankings. Dad was all the parent I had. I fixed him up.

In 1944, when I was six and Stanley was eight, the Gernhardts asked Dad to leave. Stan thinks a long railroad strike ran out Dad's money and the Gernhardts couldn't afford to carry us anymore. I remember a running argument between Dad and the Gernhardts that extended even to accusations that they were secretly steaming open his mail. Stan also seems to think that a fire he started more or less unintentionally may have forced the move. "It was near Christmas. Upstairs one day I stuck a big long curtain into a heater just to see what it would do. It caught fire and the fire went up the wall and I screamed and jumped under a bed. Dad came racing up the stairs and jerked that curtain off and stomped on it and pulled my leg out from underneath that bed and whaled me really bad. And then when we had Christmas, I think all I got for Christmas was three comic books and I was told I had not been very good that year. I think shortly after that we moved out. I think maybe they were afraid that I would set a fire or something." The Gernhardts, restored to prosperity by the war, by Mr. Gernhardt's Alaskan expedition, may have tired of boardinghouse keeping, of raising someone else's increasingly obstreperous sons. But according to Paul it was Dad who became difficult.

For whatever reasons, we left. Left Paul and Betsy, left Mr. and Mrs. Gernhardt, left Lois. Left the big elm we climbed, the limestone porches where we played, the green yard, the dining room with its mirrors regressing into infinity, the bedroom where robins sang at the windows to wake me to the day. Left— already the second time for me, and the third time, Des Moines the second, for Stanley—all we knew of home.

Thereafter we lodged to other people's profit, precariously, wherever Dad could find to go to ground.

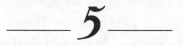
BETWEEN 1944 AND 1946, my father, my brother and I moved
four times. Stanley and I attended three different schools in
those two years. I remember only two of the four places where
we boarded. Stan identifies a third, the first after the Gernhardts'. "This woman took in day babies. Her place always
smelled like baby pee. It was a very small house. We would
always get involved—I would at least—flushing out the diapers
in the toilet. She had problems getting around. She was house-
bound a lot because of the babies. She loved Cokes. She'd give
us these coffee cans, empty Folger's coffee cans, and send us
down to the drugstore and they would fill them up with fountain
Cokes and we'd bring them back to her." Stan remembers celebrating the end of the Second World War at the baby place,
but here I think his memory compresses; my school records put
us on our third move beyond the Gernhardts' by August 1945.

The world darkened emotionally for me after we left the
Gernhardts'. I had lost my second mother, and this time I knew
my loss. Stanley withdrew as well. He made friends his own
age at school and decided I didn't need walking home. —You
know the way. We don't want a little kid hanging around.

One of Stanley's duties, self-appointed but necessary, was

disconnecting umbilicals. My brother announcing that I was old enough to tie my own shoes is my earliest memory. I was at least three. Until then he'd tied my shoes for me, or Dad or someone else had. Stanley told me he'd seen me tying my shoes on the sly when they came undone and I thought no one else was looking. He was right. I had. I staged a monumental temper tantrum then to change his mind. Will of iron: good luck. This time, condemned to walk home alone, I limited myself to crying and begging. That didn't work either.

When the last bell rang I was the first one out the door. I trailed Stanley and his friends for a few days; then they worked out how to dodge me. Forlornly I accepted my fate. I knew the way. Loneliness was the problem, not geography. I was new to the school and shy. I began reading as I walked. That made me an obvious target. One day a gang of boys ambushed me and pushed me around. From now on, they told me, they'd be waiting for me every day after school to beat me up.

I was terrified. Stanley was my only hope. I told him what had happened. At first he didn't believe me. He thought I'd made it up. He said he'd follow me and see. The next afternoon the bullies ambushed me again. I prayed silently that Stanley was behind me. He kept his word. He roared up and beat the hell out of them. That was the last time they bothered me. Stanley wasn't any bigger or older than the bullies, but he was tougher. It was a family matter. Once he'd settled it he went back to his friends and left me to walk home alone. I was proud of my independence soon enough, and on weekends I still had my brother to myself.

The loss of nurturing was harder. Books populated my desolation. Books embellished the hole to a window, worlds beyond the world where the mysteries of the world had explanations. I wandered the stacks of the neighborhood public library pulling down books. I sat on the floor of the library reading. I browsed encyclopedias. Librarians returned me to the stacks to put away books they said were too old for me.

I wanted to know how everything worked. I discovered popular science. In the first book I remember reading I flew in a rocket with a boy named David close to the surface of the sun. Before he began his tour of the solar system he was warned not to approach the sun too closely.

—Your arm alone will weigh nearly a thousand pounds, David.

—I'll be careful, Professor Jones.

Risking all to see the swirling fires, like Icarus before him, approaching the sun well within the orbit of Mercury, David barely managed to pull the lever that ignited our rocket's great engines to lift our ship away from incineration. On the moon, contrariwise, we leapfrogged like giants in the light gravity, only one-sixth Earth's. We raced out to see the rings of bright Saturn, on to swollen, angry Jupiter with its giant red spot, back to dusty Mars where the equatorial moss waxed and waned with the chilly seasons. Traveling the solar system allegorized my escape.

Stanley introduced me to *The Story of Doctor Dolittle*. One by one I read every book in the Hugh Lofting series. I identified with Tommy Stubbins, the cobbler's son in Puddleby-on-the-Marsh who became Doctor Dolittle's apprentice, but I identified more ambitiously with the doctor himself. I tried talking to animals, squirrels in particular, imitating their sounds. I fancied they understood me. Doctor Dolittle wandered the world alone and the animals gave him their uncritical devotion. I wanted to be as wise as he and as beloved.

His voyage to Africa colored my life. The first time I left the United States, in 1972, when I was thirty-five, I traveled to East Africa on assignment to write about the search for early man, a story I'd pitched. Before then, in college, Stubbins-like, I'd written to Louis Leakey impulsively offering apprenticeship. (*Dear Rhodes*, Leakey wrote back dryly, *we haven't enough jobs over here for Kenyans: stay in school.*) Before then, as a teenager, I'd read Albert Schweitzer's *Out of My Life and Thought*, drawn by his missionary work in Gabon, and determined to model my conduct on Schweitzer's ethic of reverence for life. I set my novel *The Last Safari* in East Africa, to use my experience of travel there. Its white hunter isn't a physician like Dolittle and Schweitzer, but he lives alone and teaches orphaned lion cubs to hunt. I based him in part on a tent-camp operator I met on the Serengeti up the road from Olduvai, George Dove. Dove told me the lion cub story. The Doctor Dolittle books assemble into a child's *Heart of Darkness*, don't they, a high-minded foreground set against a background dark with libido. The bare-breasted native women I discovered in the *National Geographic* and searched out in mildewed stacks in neighborhood garages fixed the connection.

Richard Halliburton's Book of Marvels carried on the Dolittle tradition for me. Halliburton was a flamboyant Princetonian who financed his exotic travels writing large-text children's books crowded with dramatic photographs. His "Dear reader" introduction must have caught my eye: "When I was a boy in school my favorite subject was geography. . . . I often said to myself: 'I wish my father, or somebody, would take me to all these wonderful places. . . .' Well, I'm grown up now. But as yet I haven't any son or any daughter to go traveling with me. And so, in their places, may I take you?" Halliburton took me to visit the Golden Gate Bridge, the Highest Waterfall (Yosemite Falls), the Deepest Canyon (the Grand Canyon), the Greatest Dam (Boulder), Niagara, New York City, Washington—exotic places then, before interstate highways—and on down to Popocatepetl and the Panama Canal. Halliburton swam the Panama Canal, braving alligators and piranhas. "I dived into its waters on the Atlantic side, and, by daily stages, swam to the Pacific—locks, lake and all—fifty miles." He commissioned himself the S.S. *Richard Halliburton* and paid his toll for passage like any other vessel, by tonnage. Since he weighed one-thirteenth of a ton, moving nine million cubic feet of water through the Canal locks cost him thirty-six cents.

Halliburton's *Second Book of Marvels* took me on from the Occident to the Orient, to the pyramids and Mecca and the Colossus of Rhodes. His photograph of the Kaaba at Mecca, a cubic temple draped with a dark camel's-hair veil, reverberated long afterward. I recognized its doppelgänger in the cubic, tar-papered sixty-foot shed that Los Alamos built at Eniwetok in 1951 to house Mike I, the first megaton-scale hydrogen bomb. But if a visual memory of Halliburton's Kaaba survived forty years with its freight of symbolism intact, I'm more struck today, looking over his books again, with his photographs of the tomb of Henri Christophe, the Black King of Haiti, and of Capri's Blue Grotto. In Halliburton's heavily airbrushed reproductions the Blue Grotto is a hole into the Mediterranean's amniotic shallows, luridly lit and vaginal. Christophe's stark white bread-loaf tomb is a violent burial, the hardened cast of the mass of quicklime in the courtyard of his fortress into which his corpse was dropped after his suicide to prevent its mutilation by his enemies. I remember lingering over both photographs in a trance.

From the baby place we moved to lodgings more like the Gernhardts', closer to middle-class: husband and wife and two children, a girl my age and her older brother, Toby. We were experimental boarders, wartime billetings, the first that the family had tried and probably the last. The furnishings were co-ordinated; lunch was more likely to be Campbell's soup than something homemade, a sign in those days of upscale aspirations; and a spinet piano occupied a place of pride in the living room. I don't understand how I pushed past my shyness to reach her, but the girl and I joined forces. All of us—Stanley, Toby, the girl and I, and probably neighbor children as well—hung out in an old black Model A body abandoned in a vacant lot near the house. For a fad that summer we took up burning discarded asphalt shingles, spelling out our names on the sidewalk in dripping tar. Sometimes Toby stole chunks of carbide from his dad, who used the compound in a hobby engine; we dropped them into back-alley puddles to generate bubbles of acetylene gas. When we lit the bubbles they exploded with a snap.

Once in the secret space between two garages, once in the upstairs bathroom, the girl and I exposed ourselves to each other. We were all of seven years old. We went farther. We lay together one day on a lawn bench in a neighbor's backyard under a cherry tree ripe with fruit, she below on her stomach, I on her back above, like nested spoons, pretending intercourse. My penis was released, but she hadn't removed her panties. Obviously we didn't know front from back, but close enough: we drowned in lust and ripe cherries, our ears roaring.

Toby saw us from an upstairs window. He'd caught us locked into the bathroom a few weeks before and tried to break down the door. He defended his sister's chastity ferociously.

He was always threatening to beat me up. Now he added the threat of telling his parents on me for the dirty things I did to his sister. She was just as eager as I.

Dad had looked long and hard for this new boarding. We had a big attic room. Except for Toby, I was happier than I'd ever known; I was in love. The girl and I had promised to find each other when we grew up. We'd secretly pledged to marry.

Too good to be true. Dad came home one day to disaster. The father and mother—"a thin, bald-headed guy," Stan says, "and she was rather thin herself"—took him aside for a whispered conference. Someone had carved a dirty word into the piano keys. The piano was a major investment. It represented hard-earned money but it also represented gentility, aspiration. Dad didn't repeat the word. If we'd done it, we'd know what it was. If we hadn't done it, we'd be better off not knowing.

The nation was fighting for democracy, but we were offered trial by ordeal. Our landlords marched their children off to the rec room in the basement. Dad marched us to the attic. He sat one of us on a hard chair in the hall, took the other into our room and closed the door. That way we wouldn't be able to coordinate our stories.

Whoever marked up the piano knew who he was, Dad warned us. He'd have to tell the truth and take his punishment like a man. If he didn't, we probably couldn't stay there anymore. They knew one of the four of us did it. Whoever it was should just go on and fess up and get it over with. If we didn't, he'd spank us one after the other until someone smartened up.

I hadn't done it and I knew I hadn't done it, but I felt as if I'd done it. The way Dad talked to me made me think that he thought I'd done it. Worse, Stanley was sure I'd done it. He fired his angriest glare across my bow when we passed each other going to and from the room. It didn't even occur to me that Toby or the girl might have done it, because I knew Stanley had done it, just as he'd taken apart his pocket watch years before. I matched him glare for glare.

I don't remember being spanked then, but I don't remember Dad ever spanking me. Stan remembers. "We were encouraged to scream real loud," he says. The fathers clumped up and down the stairs comparing notes. The first time around, Dad spanked us by hand. The next time he threatened to whip us with his belt. I was thinking seriously of confessing, just as I'd confessed to the pocket-watch crime. But something told me that scratching dirty words into the keys of a cherished piano being acquired slowly and sacrificially on the installment plan was a lot worse than taking apart a pocket watch. I kept my mouth shut.

Dad stalled at whipping us. I think by then he suspected we were innocent. He even apologized for having to punish us. —It's important we keep this place, boys. I had a hard time finding it.

I was approaching panic. I knew Stanley would never confess. We'd all be whipped bloody. Maybe I should confess after all.

Dad shook his head sadly and unbuckled his belt. He looked at me as if I'd get the first round. I was ready to take the blame even though I didn't know which dirty word I'd be claiming I'd carved. Preparing to betray my innocence, it didn't occur to me that I might have to prove my guilt. At the last minute our landlord came up and called Dad off. Toby's parents had forced him to watch his sister's spanking. Some pale flicker of altruism burned through his caul of dullness and he confessed. I felt righteously indignant in direct proportion to the volume of humiliation I'd been preparing to swallow. Toby's confession

confirmed his essential criminality. Why had I blamed Stanley?
"They brought us up a huge bowl of popcorn as a peace offering,"
Stan says, rolling his green eyes.

I caught a glimpse of the graffiti the next day: ugly and
black, cut larger than I expected, the word "FUCK." Stan thinks
there was more to the message than that. "It was 'RR' "—my
initials—"plus the little girl's initials. It was 'Richard loves so-
and-so.' And maybe the 'FUCK' too, I don't know." Given the
evidence, I'm grateful I wasn't simply convicted out of hand.
Except I wasn't stupid, and who would be stupid enough to leave
his initials permanently carved into the scene of the crime?

But the damage was done. Toby's parents still blamed us.
A working-class family had corrupted a middle-class home. The
experiment failed. Dad was soon off looking for other lodging.
I never saw the girl again. I don't even remember her name.
Back to the books.

CHAPTER

6

WE MOVED THEN to a real boardinghouse, the authentic item, fabled in song and story. An aging slattern ran it who smoked and drank and swore and sponsored loud all-night poker parties. She knew how to bread a meat loaf and how to make up a dish of chicken and gravy with barely enough wings, necks and backs to go around. When she set a platter on the dinner table how the forks would fly. Around this time Stanley and I learned a boardinghouse song. We only had to hum a bar or two at the dinner table of our new lodgings at Thirty-eighth and Michigan Avenue to tickle each other to duets of stifled giggling:

> At the boardinghouse where I live,
> Everything is growing old.
> Old cat hairs are in the butter—
> Silver threads among the gold.
> When the dog died we had sausage,
> When the cat died, catnip tea.
> When the landlord died, I left there—
> Spareribs were too much for me.

73

We were always a little hungry at the Michigan boarding-house. Weekends we got hungrier. During the week Mrs. Slattern served breakfast promptly. Saturdays, exhausted and hung over from her Friday night poker marathons, she tried to sleep until noon. Dad accepted the inconvenience and went on to work—he still worked a six-day week. Stanley and I would have been glad to drain a glass of milk and grab a stack of graham crackers and spend the morning playing outside, but barring the kitchen is the first principle of boardinghouse cost control. We were awake onward from dawn but stuck in our room waiting for breakfast. We studied our position and realized we controlled the high ground. The room Dad had taken happened to be directly above our landlady's bedroom, and the hungrier we got the less we cared how much we disturbed her. We'd read for a while, talk, get giggly, start wrestling and move on to pillow fighting and handstands against the wall. I'd roll off the bed, Stanley would roll off the bed, books and bodies would thump the floor. When Mrs. Slattern couldn't take the racket any longer she'd pound her ceiling, our floor, with the handle end of a broom. Stanley would convulse, I'd convulse, we'd shush each other, we'd climb back onto the bed and try to read. The cycle repeated. Sooner or later, acidly complaining, the woman dragged herself up.

Heading out through the stale beer and cigarette and cigar butts of the poker parlor was nauseating. Once outside we ran free. The summer of 1945 was glorious. I turned eight that summer, old enough to keep up with my nearly ten-year-old brother. "We found an old container of church keys," Stan remembers, "—beer openers—and put them on the trolley tracks and had the trolley flatten them for us. We did it so often the trolley driver finally stopped and got out and chased us

74

away. He probably thought we'd make the trolley jump the tracks." I don't remember church keys, but I remember flattening fluted steel pop-bottle caps into doubloons. I dug the disks of cork gasket from pop-bottle caps as well to make badges— the cap on the outside of my T-shirt, the gasket on the inside, press the two together and they sandwiched the shirt and stuck.

> Pepsi-Cola hits the spot—
> Twelve full ounces, that's a lot—
> Twice as much for a nickel too—
> Pepsi-Cola is the drink for you.
> Nickel nickel nickel nickel nickel . . .

We searched the neighborhood for salvage to buy candy. We discovered we could turn in pop bottles and collect the two cent deposit. In 1945 a penny would buy two miniature paraffin bottles of colored fruit syrup or a foot-long strip of paper tape stuck with dots of chocolate candy. A nickel would buy a big Baby Ruth candy bar or, my favorite, a set of sweetened, vanilla-flavored orange wax Pan's pipes the size of a pack of cigarettes. I bit the wax away from the pipes bottom up, altering their pitch, blowing and chewing, blowing and chewing in a cloud of artificial vanilla.

Mills—red and green plastic sales-tax counters—were harder to accumulate. Missouri had legislated a fractional sales tax measured in tenths of a cent. Rather than allowing merchants to round up to the next cent, which would have defeated the purpose of the tax, the state issued mills, nickel-sized plastic coins with holes in the middle like Life Savers, a red mill worth one-tenth of a cent, a green mill worth five-tenths of a cent. In

1945 grown-ups neglected mills the way people today neglect pennies. We salvaged them wherever we found them. We even walked the street gutters watching for mills the rain had washed along—their colors made them easy to spot—but they were such debased coinage that it was a good day when we collected even a nickel's worth of mills. In a pinch they served as a mediocre substitute for chewing gum. They were soft enough to bend, and flexing them fatigued them until they split into bite-sized halves. If you chewed them long and hard you could ruin them into a kind of wad.

When there was dew on the grass, mornings when we got out early, we headed for the football field at Central High School, a few blocks from where we lived. A six-foot letter C was set into the hill on the south side of the field in ceramic tile, and the dew slicked the tile to a slide. We soaked the seat of our shorts sliding down the C, but they dried across the hot summer mornings. When we got bored with sliding we searched under the wooden spectator stands for lost coins. I still remember my rage of jealousy when Stanley found most of a roll of nickels a vendor must have dropped. I'd walked past the windfall just seconds before and missed it. I called for a fifty-fifty split. "Finders keepers, losers weepers," Stanley recited. I nagged him for an hour before he deigned to grant me one and then a second nickel, exhorting me to split the next money I found with him in return. He can't have held out much hope for a payoff. I thought he had a gift for finding money. He even found a dollar once lying wadded on the sidewalk. The truth is, he could see. I was myopic, but I didn't know that until the eighth grade, when a teacher noticed I couldn't make out the blackboard even from the front row.

We were still climbers. We'd advanced from trees to billboards. We found the greatest billboard of our childhood near the Michigan boardinghouse. Raised across a corner vacant lot, it towered up freestanding two full stories into the air on a scaffolding of pine boards painted forest green. A narrow walkway projected from the billboard's lower edge. The ladder to the walkway started ten feet above the ground to discourage climbers. We took our chances with splinters and scaled the scaffolding itself. We spent hours up there above the steam of the summer streets, dangling our bare feet in space and watching people go by.

My red hair bleached copper-gold in the summer. Stanley's blond hair paled nearly white. We wore striped T-shirts and summer shorts and the summer sun deeply tanned me and innumerably freckled Stanley wherever our skin was exposed. The rest of us, our wiry shoulders, bony chests, flat bellies, skinny thighs, buttless butts and hairless little circumcised willies, our summer birthday suits, shone pinkly pale in contrast under the bare electric light above the white claw-foot bathtub where we washed away the city before bed. On Saturday nights, holy ceremony, Dad would send us in the gathering dark to the corner drugstore to buy a pint of black raspberry ice cream. We'd rush back against its melting and eat it sitting at the window of our room trying to catch a breath of breeze, sharing one spoon.

The summer of 1945 was also a bloody summer. I'd forgotten how bloody it was until I interviewed the physicist Luis W. Alvarez for my book *The Making of the Atomic Bomb*. Luie had flown as an observer in one of the two B-29s that accompanied the *Enola Gay* to Hiroshima, an assignment he'd finagled because he liked to be on the spot when history was made. The Hiroshima bomb was one of a kind and untested. Robert Oppenheimer had asked Luie to design an instrument that could measure the Little Boy blast and he'd convinced Oppenheimer that he ought to monitor the parachute gauge he devised on the mission itself.

I didn't ask Luie to justify the bombing of Hiroshima and Nagasaki, I wasn't that presumptuous, but he'd been challenged on the question often enough that he brought it up himself, turned red in the face and slapped his hand on his desk and insisted the atomic bombings were necessary as a firebreak to shock the Japanese into surrender. He had an experiment for me, he said, one he'd proposed to a group of graduate students once who'd asked him how he could justify dropping those terrible bombs on all those nice Japanese: I should go to the library and look up the last issue of *Life* magazine before *Life* carried the story of the atomic bomb and see what I found there to assess the public mood.

I looked up that issue of *Life*. I found what Luie suspected I'd find. I'd seen the issue before, in 1945, when I was eight, and remembered it. It made the hair stand up on the back of my neck. The preeminent family magazine of the day devoted a full page of photographs to the burning to death of a Japanese soldier flushed from his hiding place with a flamethrower. "The flamethrower is easily the most cruel, the most terrifying weapon ever developed," the *Life* caption writer explained innocently, a week before Hiroshima. "If it does not suffocate the enemy in his hiding place, its quickly licking tongues of flame sear his body to a black crisp. But so long as the Jap refuses to come out of his holes and keeps killing, this is the only way."

The atomic bomb was a deliverance. Almost everyone felt that in 1945, even many Japanese—a sense of enormous relief. There it was on the cover of *Life* the week after the cruel flamethrower, that first mushroom cloud, the long, narrow, dirty neck

slanting up from Hiroshima like a tornado. Stanley and I staged
our very own homegrown ticker-tape parade to celebrate the end
of the war. "We climbed up on this huge billboard," Stan says,
"—it was way up in the sky, we loved high places—we took a
whole bunch of scrap paper, tore it into little bitty bits, and we
shouted, 'The war is over! The war is over!' and threw paper all
around." But behind relief, for me at least, came revelation. I
remember staring at the photograph of the Little Boy cloud and
trying to comprehend a force compressed into one bomb that
could decimate a city. I was thoroughly stupefied with propaganda, the Japanese were monsters, I wasn't sorry for them,
they got what they deserved, but I felt in the pit of my stomach
that here was an unleashing beyond any politics, here was universal indifference to human pretension, something glossed over
in church and denied, a force of nature—abrupt, implacable,
final.

That's one point the bombs made. But even in 1945 I
understood the complement of that point as well: that nature is
far more interesting, more challenging, more profound, than
even the most ornate human construct—religion or politics or
whatever—and relentlessly honest. The mechanism of the bomb
tolerated no hypocrisy. It was built on hard evidence, not faith,
hope or charity. The science that discovered that mechanism
tolerated no hypocrisy either. I was already attracted to science,
most of all because science was a potential source of truth,
however hard, unmediated by adults—at least by any adults I
knew. Now the attraction intensified. The only model at hand,
unfortunately, was popular science. I began learning not how
to do science but how to explain it.

The large violence of the world showed itself in other ways
as well that summer. Magazines, newspapers and newsreels

reported the liberation of the Nazi death camps. Up to that point I had believed war was mostly machines fighting machines and the heroics of individual soldiers, an enlargement of our play. The death camps opened the gate to the essential slaughter. I was ashamed to look at the monstrous photographs, ashamed to take even the bare knowledge of their condition from human beings who had suffered so horribly. The propaganda I'd absorbed gave me a context in which to locate the monstrosity: here was Nazi evil revealed. That's what most of us thought; that's what the Nuremberg trials were about; but it was demeaning and misleading to discount the death camps with *ad hominem* argument. They were a far more essential manifestation of the twentieth century's destructive extremity than that. I didn't know any better.

The other violence was a partial eclipse of the sun. I'd read of its coming, on a hot summer afternoon, and I was outside with a cardboard pinhole when it began. I visualized it on my cardboard objective, the moon eating the sun. But nothing prepared me for the darkening metallic shimmer it lent to the air, for the birds flying to roost and twittering, for the neolithic fright it roused in me of the world closing down.

The death camps, the eclipse, the bomb, all spoke to my deep sense of vulnerability, alone more or less on the city streets beyond precariously rented lodging, one parent lost and only one parent left, like one kidney left or one lung, between me and the void. Stanley was a shield, not a fortress. I wanted power of my own, for protection. Raw intelligence, my basic resource, was the foundation I began building on. I understood it might elaborate eventually to wisdom, a commodity people sought and would reward. *Life* was full of science now, beginning with conceptually muddled but visually dazzling demonstrations of the principles of nuclear physics. I tore out the science articles, memorized their contents more or less, carried them to school, when school started, in a large-size cornflakes box as if they were actual sustenance and impressed my teachers and wearied my classmates with elaborate explanations of basic science at show-and-tell. No, it was worse than that. Even my teachers learned to ration my exposure, avoiding my eyes when they asked if anyone had anything to present to the class. For my part, I was eager as a recruit, wired, ready to pounce, my hand already down in the cornflakes box fingering my intellectual ammunition, deciding the caliber I'd use.

An incident that winter put my search for wisdom in perspective. I lost a library book. The librarian understandably expected me to make up the loss, a five-dollar charge. I asked Dad for the money. It was half a day's wage. He refused to pay it. He told me to find the book. I carried that message back to the librarian. The librarian sent me to the principal. She ordered me to bring the money by Friday or not to come to school.

I was afraid to ask Dad again. I'd seen a reserve of cash he kept on a shelf in our common closet, ten dollars or so. I could have stolen the money I needed to pay the fine, but I was sure he'd notice the loss. Furious and desperate that cold Friday morning, I loitered until Stanley went on to school. I stole five dollars from Dad's stash, my heart pounding, buckled on my coat and set out to run away from home. At the corner drugstore, where we bought our summer ice cream, I studied what supplies I'd need to survive on my own. I'd decided to trolley out to Swope Park, a big city park and forest reserve in southeastern Kansas City, and become a hermit. After long deliberation, furtively, I bought a box of kitchen matches and a pack of wide-line three-ring notebook paper. I could use the paper to start fires and also to keep notes.

Outside I waited for the trolley bus that connected to the

sleek electric light-rail trolley that ran out east to the park. I had the presence of mind to ask the bus driver for a transfer, to get off at the right stop and to take the right car. I was sure everyone was staring at me, but no one asked me where I was going. No one seemed to care that an eight-year-old boy was wandering the city alone when he should have been in school.

I got off at the Swope Park stop and hiked back into the park. The trees were bare under an iron overcast. The ground was patchy with snow left over from the last storm. I was going to live off the land, grow up alone, learn from the animals and from nature. When I was white-haired and old, people would hear of my wisdom and come to the woods to seek me out. I would impart to them my deep knowledge of the world. The animals would teach me.

The winter bareness revealed the memorial to Colonel Swope, the man who'd donated the park, on a hillside in the far distance. Behind the memorial would be a good place to camp. I headed in that direction, down the long hill past the zoo and on out east around the lagoon where Dad and Stanley and I had gone paddleboating. The zoo was boarded up for the winter, the animals all confined inside.

They'd search for me. Stanley would be sorry he'd been mean to me. Dad would be sad. The principal would wish she'd never tried to force me to pay for the book I'd lost. I hadn't meant to lose it. After a while they'd give me up for dead.

A colonnade backed up the statue of Colonel Swope. I approached it warily, pretending to study the statue. There was no one in sight. I ducked behind the colonnade into the open woods. Fifty feet farther up the hillside I stopped and squatted on my heels. The winter woods were quiet, no birds or animals that I could hear. I'd never been alone so far from home before.

I rubbed my mittens together to warm my hands and pulled the flaps on my cap farther down over my ears. I was already chilled. It was time to make a fire. I'd have to keep it small so that no one would see the smoke. I pulled off my mittens, wadded a sheet of notebook paper and arranged it on the ground. It seemed too valuable to waste and I wished I'd bought a newspaper instead. I pushed open the drawer of the box of kitchen matches, unhooked the cardboard clip, picked out one of the wooden matches, struck it on the strip of sandpaper along the side of the box and lit the paper. It burned with an almost invisible flame. I tried to warm my hands on it. It didn't give off much heat. I'd never in my life built a fire. Stanley and I had made stink bombs, soggy brown paper bags with garbage in them— coffee grounds, old cabbage—that we'd tried to light. They hadn't burned very well either. It was morning, late morning, but night would come and harder cold. Sometimes animals escaped from the zoo.

I'd only been there twenty minutes and my dream was in ruins. My eyes clouded with tears. The tears ran down my cheeks and made me colder. I packed up my paper and matches and stumbled back out to the streetcar stop hanging my head.

I didn't go home. I went straight to school. My teacher gave me a funny look and sent me to the principal. The principal asked me why I'd played hooky. I poured out my story. She imposed no punishment, but she still wanted me to pay for the book.

Stanley thought I'd get a whipping. Instead Dad was gentle. I think he was embarrassed to have seemed to have defied the principal's authority. I returned all of the five dollars I had left from buying the notebook paper and matches and riding the streetcar, down to the penny. Dad could light his cigarettes with the matches and I could use the notebook paper in school, so the money wasn't wasted except for the streetcar fare. He cautioned me about stealing. He gave me the money to pay the fine and I promised him I wouldn't lose any more books. I didn't understand how the problem had unknotted so easily. I could be a wise man, I could be my own father, but I'd have to find my way across childhood first.

PART

2

Arbeit Macht Frei

"He doesn't know the sentence that has been passed on him?"

"No," said the officer again, pausing a moment as if to let the explorer elaborate his question, and then said: "There would be no point in telling him. He'll learn it on his body."

—FRANZ KAFKA
"In the Penal Colony"

1

MY FATHER KNEW the woman who became my stepmother before we began boarding at her house. One evening in the winter of 1947 Dad took us to a road-show production of the Grand Ole Opry in the big Masonic temple on Linwood Boulevard, the first live entertainment I remember from childhood (having forgotten the burlesque), and it seems to me she joined us for the show, sitting on the other side of Dad, turning his head. It may be that I've conflated her bewildering debut with the honky-tonk dazzle of the Opry, with lights and flash and crowd. Since I didn't know Dad had a private life, I didn't know where this small, heavily perfumed, tough-looking woman had come from; like the road show, she might have been unloaded from a truck. Another evening Dad spruced us up and took us calling on her, not at all the normal drill in boardinghouse selection. It was obvious that he wanted us to like her. I don't think we did. After nine years of boardinghouses we had sensitive bullshit detectors, and her voice was Southern and honeyed, cunning, edged with menace.

According to my school records we moved into her house in February 1947. But memory keeps time differently from school records. I have trouble believing that all that Stanley and

I lived through in the concentration camp of our stepmother years occupied only twenty-eight months of our lives, until we were removed by the Jackson County juvenile court to the relative safety of the Andrew Drumm Institute for Boys in July 1949. Four years at least, I would have said, not two and a third. I've hardly known a day in the forty years since then when I haven't felt some emotion connected with that time. I don't mean self-pity, though I used to feel enough of that. Sympathy, usually, compassion for other suffering, rage at the careless, thoughtless and nearly universal violation of the unempowered. Several of the Hiroshima *hibakusha* whom the psychiatrist Robert Jay Lifton interviewed for his book *Death in Life* told him they sometimes fantasized the destruction of the entire human world in a nuclear holocaust. Lifton thought their fantasy expressed a wish for revenge. I suppose it did, but it may also have expressed a wish to create circumstances wherein others might appreciate their unique experience. In psychotherapy, years ago, I dreamed a pivotal dream of nuclear war—who hasn't?—dreamed mushroom clouds boiling up from Kansas City, dreamed of fleeing the doomed city eastward, of looking back over my shoulder horrified but somehow also relieved, still a survivor. You may be sure I watched the television production *The Day After* with fascination, missile trails quartering the air above the city of my birth and searing light vaporizing away history down to the bone. The rubble borrowed for the production's post-holocaust set was the wreckage of a defunct hospital where my father, three decades earlier, away from one or another of our boardinghouses for a long, frightening week, had a hernia repaired.

Anne Ralena Martin, the woman's maiden name four or five husbands prior to my father, was born in Texas in 1899, which means she was forty-eight years old in 1947, nearer than my mother would have been to my father's age of fifty-four. She was a short woman with white skin, a full head of dark hair, large breasts, "very curvy," Stan says, "very feminine"—I would have said seductive—"very giggly when she was light-hearted." She used makeup heavily, powder over a pancake base, a pucker of red lipstick, thick mascara if not false eye-lashes, and her small, usually open-toed shoes had stilt heels and platform soles to boost her height. None of this matters particularly except that she was evidently a mantrap, someone who bushwhacked husbands and cleaned them out. Dad became her plow horse; she worked him for more than fifteen years, until he died of cancer of the stomach in 1964. Stan thinks she married once more after that.

The house we moved to, at 511 South Quincy in the old northeastern section of Kansas City, Missouri, a predominantly Italian enclave then and now, was small, so small I don't understand how we all fitted in before marriage made Dad's presence in my stepmother's bedroom respectable. Other than the front porch, which has been glassed in and winterized, the South Quincy house looks the same today as it did forty years ago. A living room filled the front half of the house, running back on one side into a dining room ell. The original house had one bedroom, which abutted the dining room and incorporated the only bathroom with the only toilet. A swinging door led from the dining room to the narrow kitchen. My stepmother or a previous owner had added to this cramped tuck of rooms a sleeping porch accessible off the kitchen—probably a wartime addition, since the porch's unweighted window sashes opened with spring-loaded pins, barracks-construction style. The narrow lot sloped sharply from front to back; the basement opened onto the backyard and the sleeping porch hung out over the yard on stilts. Wooden stairs led down from the sleeping porch to the yard for a back entrance. The backyard was fenced and ended at a gravel back alley that gave access to wooden one-car garages. The backyards of the houses that faced the next street east began on the other side of the alley.

When my father was dying of cancer I wrote him a letter instead of going to see him. I didn't go to see him because to do so I'd have had to see her, and although I was married, the father of two children and twenty-seven years old, I was still afraid of her. I wrote Dad that I would tell my children about him. I meant that ambiguous benediction as a compliment. Dad or my stepmother or both of them took it the other way. They construed it to mean that I would tell my children about the abuse that he had allowed. I received a letter from him in return, ostensibly from him, voiced in the first person but in her handwriting, as if dictated. My stepmother's voice breaks through a few pages along to cite the "1000 things" we boys had done as children to "torment" her and Dad, laughing and having fun at her expense, causing her and Dad to argue, vicious little ten- and twelve-year-olds. "You just go right on and continue being self centered and selfish as I now realize you allways were," my father indicts me in my stepmother's ladylike blue ballpoint handwriting on white vellum notepaper edged with gilded scallops. "You see I am learning now of many lies you & your brother Stan have told me and made of [sic] fool out of me many times when you were growing up." I'm grateful for the letter, a cold voice from a black past, my commandant still whispering in old age, like Klaus Barbie, that Stanley and I deserved what we got.

The letter comes to mind because it reveals the living

arrangements at the South Quincy house when Dad and Stanley and I moved in: her brother and her son lodged there at the time and her brother, at least, didn't immediately move. Her son helped her buy the house on South Quincy, the letter reveals. His leaving it broke her heart, my stepmother says, damage that Stanley and I also "caused," though in fact when she moved us in as paying boarders she crowded her son out. I remember her brother's rack of clothes and dresser of belongings on the sleeping porch, his piggy bank in particular, full of tantalizing change. He was a bartender and slept by day on the army cot that Dad must have taken at night. That arrangement wouldn't have been unusual in 1947; housing was in short supply in the United States in the years immediately after the war. It didn't last long. She dislodged him, I'd guess, like her son before him, to make room for us and to assure herself some privacy. The wall between the sleeping porch and the bedroom was thin.

Life in our new boardinghouse was strange at first and even ominous—Stanley in particular was anxious with foreboding—but we weren't abused. Something was going on between Dad and this woman. It threatened us because it was new and because it seemed to take him away from us. I remember the two of them cozy in the living room on Saturday night drinking beer, Dad in an armchair or a rocker, she tucked up on the couch crocheting. That was when she giggled. Dad let me sip the bitter foam from the neck of his beer bottle and I liked it. We ran around excited until they sent us to bed. The giggling gave way to heavy breathing. They turned up the country music on the radio to mask it. I don't doubt at all that we resented the intrusion of a stranger into our arrangements. We'd had Dad to ourselves for nine years, or so I thought.

There was a natural-gas shortage in Kansas City that winter.

The temperature hovered around zero for a month; the pipeline from Texas couldn't keep up with demand. School closed. We spent those bitter days huddled in front of the small living-room fireplace burning orange crates and lath, trying to stay warm. Aunt Anne, if that's what we called her, let us play old 78-RPM records on her portable phonograph to amuse ourselves. I remember in particular a comic ballad sung in stage Cockney about a noblewoman's ghost who "walked the bloody tower" with "'er 'ead tucked underneath 'er arm." "And it's awfully, awfully awkward," the grand punch line came, "to 'ave to blow 'er *nose*—with 'er 'ead tucked underneath 'er arm." Stanley and I colored with our crayons; we sang songs—probably "Silent Night" and "Comin' In on a Wing and a Prayer"; we shivered together wrapped in an olive-drab army blanket and studied the photographs in the *Kansas City Star* of the city's enormous gasometer contracted down its supporting frame to half-mast; we waited out the cold spell and eventually returned to school.

Dad arranged to send us to the country that summer, another ominous change. I didn't want to leave him; I couldn't understand why he might not want us around. Before school was out we met the person who'd be taking care of us, a plump, jolly, irreverent woman named Gretta Schonmeier,* and I fell for her instantly and felt better about going away. She was separated from her husband or divorced. We'd be living with her and her three children—a teenaged daughter named Marcia, a son about Stanley's age named James, a younger daughter my age named Shirley.

The Schonmeiers went ahead to open up the house as soon as school let out. Stanley and I followed a few weeks later, which meant we got to ride the train unaccompanied, a three-hour

*"Schonmeier" is pseudonymous, as are this family's given names.

excursion from Union Station in Kansas City to a covered station platform outside the small town of Utica, in north-central Missouri about halfway across the state. I was fascinated with the coach-car toilet. It flushed out onto the tracks. I held down the flush lever and studied the ties racing by under the coach. The passenger section was hooked up last on the train, after the mail car, which meant I could stand out on the back platform and watch the rails receding behind me, seeming to pull the countryside after them into the point at the horizon where they met. It's odd that I didn't get trainsick. In the stepmother years I threw up in, on or out of every moving vehicle I rode except my bicycle, the one conveyance that regularly carried me away from her.

The roof over our heads that last summer before our captivity was a half-hour walk from the Utica station up a dirt country road, a one-story, two-room farmhouse with a well outside the front door drawn by a hand pump at the sink, a Coleman lantern for light, an outhouse down a dirt path for a toilet. We all slept in one room, in beds pushed against the walls, Mrs. Schonmeier and Marcia in the double bed, Stanley and James in one single, Shirley and I in another. A chamber pot in the other room served as a urinal at night. The other room was our kitchen and dining room. It let onto a good-sized yard with a picnic table. Beyond the yard a lane ambled past an abandoned chicken house to an old cemetery. Behind the house in the other direction a hillside of second-growth scrub led down to a bramble of blackberry bushes sharp with thorns.

Out of that simplicity we made a summer. After I got to know the Schonmeier children I felt better. I fell in love with Marcia. James and Stanley became buddies. They ditched me more than I liked, but Shirley was tough and game enough to

93

fill in. She kicked and flopped in her sleep. Mrs. Schonmeier cooked us hot breakfasts of muffins and eggs on a kerosene stove, suppers of fried chicken. I don't remember if we had an icebox, nor where we might have gotten the ice; it seems to me we used evaporated milk.

The railroad was our theme park, admission free. We learned the train schedule and walked the rails to the station to watch the mailbags loaded and unloaded. We followed out the spurs where freight cars were sided. When there was no one around to warn us away we swarmed over the big cars, admired their great wheels, climbed their ladders, breathed their complex aroma of rust and tie creosote and lubricating oil. I remember once hoisting myself up onto the open rim of a gondola car. The polished steel interior sloped dangerously inward and down. To avoid it I leaned too far out and slipped and fell outside headfirst toward a dangerous rail. In midair time abruptly slowed until I seemed suspended. I had leisure to think, and what I thought was that I'd better do something or my head would be crushed. What I did was grab a steel rod projecting from the coupling coming up below and spin around the rod and land on my feet in the gravel roadbed with no more damage than abrasions on my arms and a good scare. After that I stayed away from gondola cars.

Stanley and I scaled up our flattening projects to match the capacity of the heavy trains. Instead of church keys or pop-bottle caps we started laying tree branches across the tracks. When the big diesel engines easily crushed those, we escalated to bigger branches and finally to a good-sized log. The Schonmeier children watched with us from a siding to see what would happen to the log. What happened was that the engineer blasted his horn, hit the emergency brake and screeched the train to a halt. We were so amazed we forgot to hide. A brakeman came running to clear the obstacle. We pretended to be innocent bystanders, balancing in a line along a spur rail and whistling to the air as if the log had jumped onto the track by itself. The brakeman chewed us out royally. "You could have derailed the damned train," he told us, and swore us off further sabotage. We didn't admit that we'd done it, but we promised we never would again.

James extracted a box turtle from the dung of the outhouse and we scrubbed it down and made it a pet for a day—at night it crawled off. We picked blackberries and ate them sugared with milk. One day Mrs. Schonmeier made All-Bran muffins to use up a staling box of cereal. I'd never tasted anything so fine. I stuffed nine of them at a sitting slathered with butter and jelly and spent the next two days trotting off to the outhouse. I didn't like sitting out there over that open hole. If box turtles found their way in, what else might crawl there among all the curious varieties of human excrement? Mrs. Schonmeier wasn't overly concerned for my condition; it was self-limiting. "I wondered if you'd bit off more than you could chew," she twinkled.

Sometimes after supper we used the cemetery for a playground, hiding behind the tombstone slabs and riding horsey on the granite cylinders. We felt safe so long as we stuck together, so long as there was still the least evening light, but no one wanted to stay on after dark or to be the last to leave. I remember scrambling over the fence convinced a ghost was pulling on my foot, trying to hold me back. Maybe it was a morning-glory vine; maybe it was Stanley. So many stars shone in the night sky above the lane in the country darkness, they converged so strongly on the wide band of the Milky Way, that space seemed to be rushing away from us as the countryside had rushed away from the coach-car platform where I'd stood watching on the trip out from Kansas City.

Holed up in the house one restless rainy day, bored with checkers, bored with winding up the great-horned gramophone, Shirley and I played peek-down-your-panties until Mrs. Schonmeier chuckled to us to quit. Mrs. Schonmeier produced an antique Easter egg from somewhere that day. It was a hundred years old, she said. It had a dry, spooky rattle that occupied our imaginations for at least an hour. Other days I climbed the peach tree in the front yard, avoiding a nail sticking out of its trunk by pulling myself directly into the low primary fork. I fell once, ran the nail through my lip and managed to land on my feet still impaled. I squatted there screaming bloody murder until Mrs. Schonmeier came running out to extract me, lifting my lip off that cruel peg. James and Stanley teased me for mumbling, but the meaty hole the nail made impressed them.

The bright thorium mantle of the Coleman lantern that we pumped up after dark attracted bugs. June bugs came first, dive-bombing the door screen. Walking sticks followed in midsummer. James convinced me that walking sticks were poisonous. At high season they covered our door and window screens solidly shoulder to shoulder, hundreds and hundreds of them like twigs with legs, glowing green in the lantern light, looking in on our evening, watching us. I stuck close to Mrs. Schonmeier and the Coleman, terrified that we might be overrun. On the Fourth of July, my birthday, we unbraided pigtails of firecrackers and spent the day blasting every crevice we could find. Harassing the gauzy colonies of bagworms that hung from the trees like clouds of swallows' nests was cruel sport, but they could ventilate the entire crown of an elm and kill it, and they seethed in rewarding commotion when the explosion blew through. Fireflies we collected by the jarful and cherished.

During the week we washed to the milder baptismal doctrines of sprinkle and pour, but Saturday night was bath night and ordained full immersion. We boys hauled in the galvanized steel washtub. Mrs. Schonmeier heated water on the stove to fill the bath. We waited our turn in the bedroom with the door shut, a second, kerosene lantern for light. Beautiful Marcia got to bathe first while the water was pristine. We might have tried to peek, but Shirley would have snitched. After Marcia Mrs. Schonmeier supervised us each in turn, personally washing our hair and our ears, changing the water three bathers along. I think she bathed last, Marcia baby-sitting, the only moment of privacy the poor woman had all week. With my crew-cut hair damp and my body clean and cool, with the moan of distant trains to lull me, I sank into sleep those Saturday nights like a stone into the depths of the sea.

Sunday morning we put on clean clothes and walked up the road to a white clapboard church. Ribbed paper fans in the pew racks beside the black hymnals advertised the local funeral home. We sang hymns fanning ourselves against the heat of Missouri summer, a mother out of Frans Hals and five shining, tanned children. The local people discreetly looked us over. I still wore shorts that summer. Stanley and James were old enough for jeans, the loose kind, unfashionable now, that farmers wear. For dress occasions like church we had cotton shirts Mrs. Schonmeier made for us from promotional flour sacks. She let us pick out our favorite flower patterns at the general store. One by one we ate our way to country chic through her glorious biscuits and pies.

Dad was supposed to come and see us one hot August Saturday. Mr. Schonmeier arrived ahead of him on the morning train. Mrs. Schonmeier's husband trudged up the road carrying a grocery sack of bottled beer. He had a long face like a horse and he was sunburned dark red down to his shirt collar. He'd come to tear out a rotten section of the kitchen wall and replaster it. He took off his shirt, opened his first beer and worked and drank through the morning and early afternoon. Stanley slipped outside from watching him and whispered to me that Mr. Schonmeier was sweating blood. I snuck in to see. His sweat did look pink, pale pink, like the ooze from a blister. It beaded on his white back and ran down his spine into his pants and stained the edge of his shorts. So people really did sweat blood.

Her husband's visit upset Mrs. Schonmeier. She was nervous all morning. He didn't know that Dad was coming out the same day. Mrs. Schonmeier finally told him and he started swearing at her. She shooed us outside to play in the yard. We tried to play, but we could hear them arguing and needed to listen.

The afternoon train went by. Half an hour later Dad walked up the lane. He was wearing his gray work pants and a dressy white short-sleeved shirt with a diamond pattern woven into it. I ran up to hug him, feeling rescued. Stanley stood back a little, too proud to show his need. Dad gathered him in. I started chattering away. Then Mr. Schonmeier came out of the house with a butcher knife.

"You son of a bitch," he challenged Dad, heading Dad's way, "you think you can sneak out here and get to my wife. I knowed what you was up to from the very start." Dad deliberately put us behind him. We backed away to give him room.

Mrs. Schonmeier ran out from the house. "That's a lie!" she called to her husband. "I told you he just come out to see his boys!"

Mr. Schonmeier didn't take his eyes off Dad. "I knowed what you come out for," he sneered. "You come out for a little nooky, ain't you fella?"

They started circling. Dad moved backward to the picnic table and around to the other side. "Listen," he told Mr. Schonmeier, "I just come out here to see my boys. I didn't mean you no harm. You ought to put that knife away before you get in trouble."

"Shit," Mr. Schonmeier jeered, "you afraid? This here knife scare you a little? You're the one in trouble, sneaking out here trying to steal someone's wife. You going to fight or you going to be chickenshit and run away?" Mrs. Schonmeier had circled past the two men at a safe distance. She moved us all to the far end of the yard.

"I don't want to fight you," Dad said. I was afraid for him, but I was also embarrassed. I'd seen too many movies—I thought he ought to fight. He kept watching the knife and moving around the table to stay away from Mr. Schonmeier.

Mr. Schonmeier swung the knife across the table in slow circles. "You bastard," he taunted Dad again. "You afraid of someone who's a real man?"

Stanley broke away then from Mrs. Schonmeier and ran into the house. When he came out a second later he had two more knives. He ran around to Dad's side of the table and passed one to him. He brandished the other one himself. My father and my brother confronted Mrs. Schonmeier's threatening husband side by side.

He stared at them dumbfounded. It took him a while. Then he shrugged, defeated. "Shit," he said, "I ain't going to fight no kid." He turned his back on them and walked into the house. We heard the knife clatter to the floor. He reappeared dragging his shirt and headed off down the lane. "You can have it," he called back bitterly over his shoulder, words to that effect. "It ain't no good to me no more."

At the end of August, when we expected to go home, Mrs.

Schonmeier revealed that we'd be staying on into the fall. She explained vaguely that Dad and Aunt Anne needed more time to make arrangements for us, whatever those might be. I was happy living with the Schonmeiers, but I missed Dad, and starting over at yet another school was disheartening. I worried that Dad was abandoning us. Stanley reassured me. Dad would never do that.

Mrs. Schonmeier enrolled us in a one-room country school. Each of seven grades was assigned a row of desks. The desktops had built-in inkwells for the steel-nibbed pens with which we outfitted ourselves at the general store. As intruders from the city we were morally suspect, fair game for the farm kids, and I don't think the spinster teacher liked my know-it-all performances at show-and-tell, because after the first few she stopped calling on me entirely. Our playground was a pasture. Near the schoolhouse hornets had dug a nest in the ground. Two big farm boys, bored with school, tore the nest open one day at recess. The hornets drove everyone screaming indoors. I've retained two lessons I learned at that country school. A country classmate informed me authoritatively that mixing aspirin with Coke would kill you, and until adulthood I never did. And the teacher instructed us when we rubbed our eyes always to rub around the eyeball with a circular motion. If we rubbed across the eyeball itself, she said, we'd ruin our vision. Mine was already compromised. I must have been rubbing wrong.

A farm boy my age befriended me. He lived within walking distance of our cabin in a regular house with indoor plumbing and electric lights. His parents kept decorative guinea hens that crowed raucously as they settled in the trees around the house at dusk to roost. One of the farm cats had started a project of killing them. My friend's parents ordered him one evening, casually, as farm people do, to take the cat out and kill it. He was afraid. I promised him I'd help him. He picked up the cat, a small calico, and we walked out together down the darkening lane. We wondered how you kill a cat. It had teeth and claws; how did you kill it? We came upon a plow. "We could bash it against the plow," my friend said. I said I'd hold it if he'd take its back feet and start swinging. I held it. He took the legs. I said, "Move over closer," and he said, "Okay, I'm ready, let go!" and he swung the cat and it screamed and its head hit the sharp steel plowshare tunk! and the cat screeched and tore itself out of his hands with the back of its head laid open. It flopped on the ground still alive and crawled and clawed at the dirt of the lane to get away but it couldn't use its hind legs. We both started crying and my friend grabbed the cat by its hind legs and lifted it up and swung it against the steel share again tunk! and the body went limp and he dropped it. I grabbed him and screamed and threw him down and fell on him and tried to hit him and then we were holding one another for comfort and crying.

We walked back to the farmhouse holding hands without saying anything. When we went into the living room my friend's mother said, "Did you kill that cat?"

My friend said, "Yeah."

His father was drinking a beer. His face was flushed. He looked at me and grinned. "Richard," he asked me, "what's the wettest vegetables in the garden?"

I told him I didn't know.

"Lettuce, turnip and pea," my friend's father said. "Get it? Lettuce, turnip and pea!"

"Lonnie, that's enough," my friend's mother said.

"It was only a joke," my friend's father said. The scolding

annoyed him. He looked at me as if I'd caused it and dismissed me. "It's time you ought to be getting home, isn't it, little man?"

We went home to Kansas City, to the house on South Quincy, in October. Dad sat us down with Anne, Aunt Anne ("She wasn't my aunt," says Stan; "even 'Aunt Anne' stuck in my throat") and told us nervously that they'd been married. That's what the summer had been about. "We're a whole family again," Dad said.

"You can call me Mother now," our father's wife told us. She must have seen the look on our faces. She smiled a cold, triumphant smile. "Your dad's let you run wild," she said. "We'll get along just fine just as soon as you two learn that we have a few rules around here."

2

STAN USES POLITICAL TERMS to describe what happened to us across the next two years at our stepmother's hands. I went out to Idaho, where he lives, to disentomb these memories with him. He spoke of force and power and domination, of rebellion and uprisings. I'd never thought of our victimization that way before. For me what happened was first of all existential. To manipulate and to tame us, to make us new men, our stepmother—we never did call her Mother, nor did she ever even remotely deserve the name—self-righteously attacked our mental and bodily integrity. She tinkered sadistically with control worked out on the surface and the interior of our bodies. I don't believe she began with a calculated program of coercion, any more than the Nazis began with a calculated program beyond expulsion for the European Jews. The problem was to deal with them, but once they'd been stripped of their rights, everything became possible. Since we were children, and had few rights in the first place, since our father was too cowardly to defend us from brutalization, everything became possible for her as well.

I think she was less violent at the outset than later—she would at least have had to test Dad's limits—but it's hard to remember when bad went to worse. Our stepmother lived by rigid systems of rules within a world of rigid and correspondingly brittle boundaries; to transgress even the least of those rules might detonate an outburst of rage that even to a ten-year-old seemed grossly disproportionate to the provocation (or it might not—the capriciousness was part of the terror). So we scrambled to learn all the rules at once.

Some were simple. She immediately assigned us to clean the house. If, cleaning the bathroom, we found that a new roll of toilet paper needed to be installed, we should install it so that it fed out under, not over, the roll. Flooded with panic, as I soon came to be in her presence, I had endless trouble mastering that arrangement, especially since once the new roll was mounted, the spindle was difficult to release, so that if I got it backward I was usually stuck struggling with it until she arrived to inspect. The first time or two that happened she wrote off as stupidity; thereafter she assumed I was reversing the toilet paper deliberately and willfully to defy her, a far more serious crime.

Much more complex, hopelessly complex, were her rules about left- and right-handedness. "You couldn't use your left hand as a dominant hand," Stan remembers, "when you were right-handed. We couldn't shovel snow in a left-handed way when we were supposed to shovel in a right-handed way. We couldn't sweep in a left-handed way when we were right-handed. There was a whole array of lists that she had that we couldn't do because it was left-handed." It's natural in manual labor to trade off hands, to sweep left and then right, to shovel right and then left, to alternate the fulcrum hand and rest the muscles that move the load. These adjustments our stepmother forbade, which by itself might have been no more than an amusing eccentricity, like the motion-studied house rules of the Gilbreth family in *Cheaper by the Dozen*, except that she enforced her interdictions with violence.

Once, for example, she and Dad had an argument that ranted on into the night, so that I fell asleep to it, and was still raging in the morning when I waked. I could see into the kitchen from my upper bunk bed on the sleeping porch. I opened my eyes to Dad standing bareass naked at the stove frying eggs. It was strange to see him naked, especially since he wasn't circumcised, and I pretended to be asleep while I peeked at him. My stepmother swung through the kitchen door then in her bathrobe. "Aren't you ashamed to be walking around naked in front of your children?" she challenged Dad contemptuously.

"Why should I be ashamed?" he threw back. "You tell me I'm not a man. Let them see for themselves."

"You're a dirty bastard," she told him. "You ought to get some clothes on."

"I'll get my clothes on when I'm damned good and ready," Dad blustered.

She grabbed the boiling teakettle off the stove and brandished it. "You son of a bitch," she shouted at him, "you think you can push me around? You go get some clothes on or I'll scald your ugly prick!"

Dad stared at her. He believed her. He hung his head and walked out. She took over at the stove.

After a while I heard the front door open and close, Dad leaving for work. She leaned into our room. "It's time to get up now," she spat at us. She assumed we were awake and listening. Her violence was partly histrionic, an exhibitionism it was obvious she enjoyed. It made her the center of attention. "Hurry it up. You can eat these eggs your goddamned father left." Stanley had slept through the teakettle business. He looked at me wondering what was going on. I shook my head to warn him.

We got dressed and sat down at the breakfast table and tried to eat our eggs. "You little brats," she started up out of the blue, "you and your son-of-a-bitch father don't know what a home is. Here I take you in and give you a good home and look at the grief it causes me." She was banging dishes in the sink and sniffing. Stanley and I kept our eyes on our plates. When our forks stopped clicking she said, "If you're done, get the hell down to the basement and start cleaning it out. I want that basement clean as a whistle today and I'd better not catch you loafing."

We marched to the basement—cement floor; rough limestone walls, walls that confined now rather than sheltered—and began loading trash into the cardboard boxes she'd saved from groceries. She strolled down to watch us. She got interested in the mason jars of canned goods she'd put up that lined the dusty raw pine shelves along the walls. There were even jars of eggs she'd preserved in glycerin. "Some of these are years old," she said to herself. She got a box and started throwing in jars of beans and pickles and beets, absently at first, then warming to the work, smashing them into a mess of bloody vegetables and zinc lids and broken bluish glass. Every time I heard another smash I jumped.

"Stanley," she ordered when she was done, "go get the mop and bucket." Stanley went upstairs and came back with the string mop and galvanized bucket we used to mop the sleeping porch and kitchen linoleum. She had him fill it at the wash sink and pour in some Lysol, a smell I still hate. "Now I want you to take turns mopping this floor," she told us, "and I want every speck of dust cleaned up."

Stanley leaned over the bucket and began to wring out the mop. He might as well have thrown a grenade. "Not *that* way, you shitty little brat!" she exploded. "Don't you know how to

106

wring out a mop?" She grabbed the mop from his hands and hauled it up to bash him with it. A big bolt stuck out where the mop head attached to the handle. The way she was holding the mop, the bolt might hit Stanley in the back of the neck and paralyze him or kill him. I froze, trying to make myself invisible. Her face contorted with rage and she bashed Stanley on the head with the metal rack of the mop. The bolt missed. He covered his head with his hands and she hit him again, swearing at him, red in the face, exultant, and then she looked around at me and saw that I saw her excitement and something clicked and she put the mop down.

"Get over here," she gritted to me. I came over beside the bucket. It was like walking up to a cobra. But her rage had collapsed back within bounds. "Now, I'll show you both once more how to wring out a mop," she went on as if nothing had happened, "and if I ever have to show you again you'll know why." She demonstrated, the water running back into the pail in a braided stream. "You dip it in the water and take it in your hands and you wring it out by twisting it to the *right*, like this, not to the *left* the way Stanley was doing it. Do you see?"

Stanley said, "Yes, ma'am," and I said, "Yes, ma'am." We'd learned to say "ma'am."

"Then next time do it right," she finished. She pointed to the jars she'd broken. "Clean up that mess too," she said casually. "I'm going upstairs."

When I reminded Stan of that early lesson in handedness, a few years ago, he looked at me for a while and then just shook his head. "You've got it turned around," he said with the authority of an older eyewitness. "It wasn't me she was beating with the mop. It was you."

We didn't often have eggs for breakfast, but our stepmother coarsened our rations before she cut them. I don't remember hunger at first. I remember kneading sealed bags of cold white oleomargarine until my hands hurt to disperse a capsule of yellow dye uniformly throughout the one-pound mass, an inconvenience the dairy industry gerrymandered from the government after the war to protect butter from direct competition. I remember being nagged whenever we asked for a second glass of milk. Milk was for babies, our stepmother contended; it wasn't good for us now that we were growing boys. She didn't want the expense. She substituted powdered milk for fresh, a chalky bluejohn she could stir up for pennies a quart. It amused her that we didn't like the taste. I remember going to school with the one sandwich she allowed us dabbed with acrid green mint jelly because she happened to have a jar on hand and wanted to use it up. I remember dinners of bread and gravy, the soft white bread bought stale at half price from the Manor Bakery's day-old store, torn into bite-sized pieces and piled on the plate, the cream gravy she slathered over the bread laced nauseously with cayenne. But those were still the days of butter- (or oleo-) and-white-sugar sandwiches, dense and sweet as white chocolate. Those were still the days of warm cherry pie sometimes for dinner, which I loved then and love now, and I was capable of almost any degree of obsequiousness before her in pursuit of a second helping, to Stanley's understandable disgust.

We went traveling. I'm not sure why. Not as reward for good behavior. Maybe to improve our outlook, probably because she couldn't leave us home alone. Dad's years of working for the Missouri Pacific had earned him a lifetime family pass good on any railroad in the country. He usually had to stay behind to work. She dragged us along. We went south, possibly to New Orleans, the train stopping when it crossed into Mississippi so the colored people could move to separate cars. "I accidentally on purpose went to the back car where all the black people were sitting," Stan remembers, "and it was dingy and dark and all the black people were looking at me and I thought, What in the world is going on here?" We went to Galveston, where I first saw the sea crashing against the breakwater. We went to Colorado Springs, where Stan remembers buying a parquet ruler assembled from twelve different kinds of wood. That was in the winter, one of the two winters we lived with her, possibly the second. "Froze our butts off," says Stan of Colorado Springs.

Wherever we went, I got trainsick. "This was another reason for her to be furious," Stan adds, "only she couldn't hit you on the train, so she would just seethe and seethe. She'd grab you and say, 'You don't *have* to be sick!'" I would stand with a churning stomach outside the one toilet at the end of the coach car, hoping that whoever was inside would finish and unlock the door and make way before I vomited. Sometimes they did; sometimes they didn't, and I vomited shamefully on the floor, my stepmother staring out the window, pretending she didn't know me. A little relieved, I'd wipe my face, take a drink of water from the fountain to clear my mouth of the taste of vomit and return to my seat. After a while a black porter would appear and she would send me up to him with a quarter tip. I felt a double humiliation at that ceremony, mine in having to acknowledge that I was responsible for the vomit, the porter's for having to clean it up.

While America rolled by in its glory out the window, we'd sit opposite her miserably trying not to wiggle, watching her crochet. She was a champion at crochet; she turned out piles of doilies and collars and antimacassars and cuffs. I'd have read a book and been happy, but reading made me sicker. Stanley and I stared and giggled, wiggled and stared. The cars must have been wired for sound, because I remember once listening to what I thought was a dumb song, a country song about "seven years with the *wrong* woman," giggling about it with Stanley and then noticing that our stepmother was dabbing at her eyes. She caught us giggling and shot us a wounded glare. "What would *you* know about it?" she snarled. She must have been transposing the gender, remembering one or another of her marriages. I was glad to see that something could hurt her, but I sure as hell knew better by then than to let my satisfaction show.

We were given to understand that everyone pulled his weight at 511 South Quincy. We couldn't just laze through childhood expecting other people to pay our way. Besides our household chores there were all sorts of jobs we could do to help support the family. She'd take half of what we made to contribute to our room and board. The rest she'd hold in safekeeping for us so it wouldn't burn a hole in our pocket. We'd need it to buy our own clothes. We could have a quarter a week for spending money. Any more than that and we'd just get into mischief.

She and Dad bought an old car that first fall. She sold Avon products and put the car to good use ferrying orders. It made possible outings to the country on Dad's days off. Our stepmother strip-mined the countryside. We were her shovels.

Some outings we collected bottles. She and Dad let us out on a likely stretch of two-lane country road. Each with a bushel basket, Stanley took one shoulder, I took the other. The car drove slowly ahead. We gathered pop and beer bottles until our baskets were full, ran forward to empty them into the trunk of the car, ran back to continue collecting. When we filled the trunk we loaded the floor and the backseat. At noon we stopped for a roadside picnic ("hoboing-type," Stan categorizes), built a small fire, heated a can of baked beans, roasted canned Vienna sausage on green sticks Dad cut with his pocketknife. Stanley and I each got one Vienna sausage, half the size of a hot dog, against the miles of stoop labor. "I can remember being so cold in my hands," Stan says bitterly, "so frozen, you know, just ready to get back in that car. They'd drive the car way, way up, where we had to walk up to it. And being just as hungry as I could be." We filled the backseat to the windows and rode home rolling in a surf of muddy bottles, the smoke of Dad's cigarette or cigar blowing back to nauseate me, our stepmother's hand swiping around to pinch or smack us if we complained. At home over the next week Stanley and I washed all those bottles, washed out the crickets and rotten mice, sorted them into boxes and wheeled them in our wagon to grocery stores to collect the two-cent refund if we could. Our stepmother counted the bottles before we left and counted the money when we got back to make sure we didn't cheat her. The arrival of cases of bottles at their counters didn't endear us to grocers. "Some of them were really adamant that they were not going to give us money for certain bottles," Stan remembers. "One got so tired of seeing us that he decided, 'You kids are not welcome here. We won't take any more of your bottles.' "

That was one kind of outing. On another we applied our climbing skills gathering bittersweet, the common country vine that matures clusters of hard red-orange berries that split open like small flowers. People use it in winter floral displays. When we spotted a bittersweet vine growing up a roadside tree or telephone pole Stanley boosted me to the berry clusters and I cut them down. Our stepmother taught me the hard way to leave the stems long.

On bittersweet outings we also hunted up black walnut trees. Black walnuts were a favorite ingredient in the Middle West for fudge and they were rarely available in grocery stores. "We stole the black walnuts," Stan says. "She'd send us over to these black walnut trees and tell us to hurry, hurry, hurry. We'd go up into the tree and shake down the nuts and gather them as quickly as we could and get out of there. We were raiding farmers' black walnut trees. We brought home sacks and sacks of black walnuts. We'd take those sacks into the basement and sit on that cold basement floor and mash off the hulls with bricks and then let the nuts dry. And then at a later time we'd take a hammer or a stone and crack them open, pick the meats out and fill up jars with them." The hulls stained our hands purplish black, an unwashable stain that had to wear away.

The black walnuts, the bittersweet and our stepmother's crocheting we sold at night from door to door. She favored apartment houses for our canvassing. Bittersweet assembled in our home factory was a dime a bunch. Mason jars of black walnuts went for several dollars, which no one would pay; eventually she had us put up the pungent nutmeats in little plastic packs that sold for thirty-five cents each. I was mortally shy in those years, shy almost to the point of catatonia, but I learned to work my way down the halls of apartments knocking on doors, pitching my odd assortment of wares, keen to the warmth of rooms and voices and the range of cooking smells. Elderly ladies sometimes bought a bunch or two of bittersweet. I don't remember selling nuts, and have taken Stan's word about that trade. Doilies sold worst of all. Doilies were treacherous. Some of the elderly ladies would invite me in ostensibly to look over my samples of crocheting when what they really wanted, I came to understand, was a chance to talk to another human being, even a scruffy ten-year-old, for a few minutes that day or week or month ("If they show any interest at all," our mean-mouthed sales training manager coached us, "tell them you have a *complete selection available* in the car"). Doilies demonstrated that

Gresham's law also applies to the coin of time: if someone bought even one piece of crocheting then I had a major sale and I was home free, but time spent demonstrating doilies was time away from selling bittersweet and walnuts. Doily time was bad time; in the worst case it might result in no sales at all that night, which meant enduring a long harangue back at the car if not hard slaps and a twisted arm. I might have sold more crocheting if I'd been properly briefed. I couldn't tell one lacy, ivory-colored piece of interlocking string from another and I had only the vaguest idea what they were for. Unconsciously, Stanley and I both probably sabotaged crocheting sales; we saw our step-mother's disappointment when a week went by and no one bought her handiwork. Treacherous little ten- and twelve-year-olds we were, just as she suspected. She taught us to hate her first of all through our bellies and our backs.

Once, on a hot summer night near the nine o'clock deadline when I was supposed to return to the car, not one bunch of bittersweet or one pack of nuts sold, much less an extravagant $2.98 doily, I knocked on an apartment door and heard movement inside. I waited and knocked again. No one answered. I began to panic. I knew there were people on the other side of the door. They were my last chance to sell something. If I came back empty-handed I'd suffer for it. I knocked again, waited another minute and then kept on knocking, deluding myself that whoever was inside somehow hadn't heard. A beefy man in an undershirt and just his undershorts threw open the door. His face was red. He twisted my shirt collar in one big hand and picked me up off the floor. I could see a woman inside buttoning her blouse. "Don't you know enough to leave people alone when they don't answer the door?" he bellowed at me. "You god-damned little punk, I ought to belt you one." I thought he was going to; I went limp with terror. He shook me like a rat. "You get the hell out of here and don't never come back!" He dropped me and slammed the door in my face. Running down the hall, spiraling down the stairs two and three at a time, frightened as I was, I was kicking myself for not trying to sell him something.

"She saw in us a way to make more money," Stan says. "To increase her income. She saw us as a business opportunity. Just to work us and work us." Besides harvesting the countryside and selling door-to-door we shoveled snow. "There was one winter," Stan remembers, "when I was shoveling snow like a fury and bringing home the money and she was pocketing all the money that I brought home. At that time I determined that I was going to cheat"—he thought of what he did as cheating— "and keep some of that money for myself, because she wasn't giving it back. She said that we would get a percentage, but it didn't work out that way." I wonder why she even bothered to pretend. I don't think the woman had a conscience. Was bait a more effective way to control us than brutality alone? "So I remember one day," Stan goes on, "I had shoveled about eighteen dollars' worth of snow at thirty-five cents a sidewalk—you can imagine how many sidewalks that was" (it would have been, roughly, fifty) "—and I determined I was going to keep out about eight dollars. I turned in about ten to her, and she was very happy. She said, 'Well, this will go into savings,' and this and that. So I knew I had eight dollars. And she never found out." I remember shoveling snow, remember the pleasure of it at the beginning after a day in an overheated classroom, the white cold of the snow and how the shovel cut it sharply into blocks and how supple and strong my back felt levering the loads of snow over my shoulder into the yards. But I got cold across an afternoon of shoveling, my gloves soaked, my feet slowly numbed to clubs in their uninsulated galoshes, I came home exhausted with less earnings than my stepmother expected of me and got sent out again supperless to find more walks to shovel, shoveling until long after dark and then bread and gravy or worse and exhausted to bed. Opportunity knocks, she explained to us zealously; the early bird gets the worm.

Besides shoveling snow, says Stan, we collected foil. "We had to tear the foil off of wrappers. Chewing gum and cigarette packs. We got big balls of it. We'd try to sell it for scrap. Get a few pennies for it." Besides collecting foil we were supposed to go from door to door on weekends and during the summer asking for work. Without props, without bunches of bittersweet or packs of black walnuts or a shovel, I found soliciting nearly impossible to do. At best I knocked and mumbled my offer with one foot already advancing backward down the porch. I didn't rustle up much work on my own, nor did Stanley. We drifted off to play and came home empty-handed. I'm not sure our stepmother expected more. I think she wanted us to understand that we were on duty twenty-four hours a day, like conscripts. That meant we were effectively AWOL whenever we converted our time to our own purposes, perpetually derelict and perpetually indictable.

Yet I must have been inspired to believe that work would set me free, because the first December on South Quincy I took up selling on my own. A mail-order company offered Gilbert chemistry sets as prizes for selling out a full selection of greeting cards. If I could peddle bittersweet and black walnuts, I reasoned, much less doilies, it ought to be a cinch to sell Christmas cards in December. I sent off for the extra-large selection that promised the largest chemistry set. It arrived in mid-December on a cold, snowy day. I started out canvassing as soon as I got home from school and did my chores. I sold up through the Northeast district toward Cliff Drive, the bluff where we'd walked down with Dad to see the Missouri Pacific roundhouse. I worked both sides of the street, hit the librarians at the branch library at Northeast High School, sold retired couples, widows, young mothers with babies in their arms. I didn't stop for supper. I was determined to sell my entire consignment of cards that day so that the chemistry set would arrive in time for Christmas. Had they all been Christmas cards that would have been easy to do, but some of them were everyday cards—cards for birthday, friendship, graduation. My sales pitch emphasized convenience. Buy now, I argued, and save a trip to the store.

Peace on earth, goodwill to men. I sold my last card at a quarter to nine. Joyfully I started home, counting my money. I came up a dime short. Stumbling, my heart pounding, I counted again and came up a dime short again. Somewhere in twenty or thirty dollars' worth of sales I'd lost a dime. I wiped my nose on my coat sleeve. There was no place on earth where I could ever get a dime. I had to get one. Any cards that weren't paid for had to be sent back. If everything wasn't sold I wouldn't win a chemistry set.

The library was just up the street. It was still open. It stayed open until nine. The librarians would help me. Librarians always helped me. I hurried to the warm library. A few grown-ups were finishing checking out. I squared off at the desk of the reference librarian who'd bought a card from me before. She looked up kindly at me. I blurted my story and asked her for a dime to replace the one I'd lost.

I learned that night the contempt people reserve for beggars. She gave me the dime and a scathing lecture. I went home ashamed but relieved. It hadn't even occurred to me to ask Dad or my stepmother to make up the dime.

SLAPPING US, kicking us, bashing our heads with a broom handle or a mop or the stiletto heel of a shoe, slashing our backs and the backs of our legs with the buckle of a belt, our stepmother exerted one kind of control over us, battery that was immediately coercive but intermittent and limited in effect. We cowered, cringed, screamed, wrapped our poor heads protectively in our arms, danced the belt-buckle tango, but out of sight and reach we recovered our boundaries more or less intact. The bodily memory of the blows, the heat of the abrasions, the caution of pain, the indignation and the smoldering rage only demarcated those boundaries more sharply. More effective control required undermining our boundaries from within. As diseases do, our stepmother sought to harness our physiology to her own ends. Compelling us to eat food we didn't like—cayenne gravy, mint jelly, moldy bread—is hardly more coercion than most parents impose, not that custom justifies it. Our stepmother tinkered more radically with manipulating what we took into our bodies and what we expelled. The techniques she developed led eventually to a full-scale assault.

Colds and tonsillitis frequently kept us home from school and underfoot. To help prevent that inconvenience she might have improved our diet. Instead she began dosing us mornings with cod-liver oil. Stanley swallowed it down. It nauseated me. It tasted like bad fish. I clamped my jaw and balked. Even her jerking and slapping didn't always prevail. She had to stop pounding me to move the tablespoon of oil to my mouth and by then I'd clamped my jaw again. Every morning was a fight. Goaded by stalemate, she devised an alternative. I loved school. It was my escape into the wide world. She fettered that love to my daily dose of oil. She forbade me to go to school until I'd swallowed it. I resisted until the last possible moment and then gagged it down.

We polished off the cod-liver oil. She remembered a bottle of mineral oil left over in the bathroom closet. She must have thought the two oils were equally invigorating. She substituted one for the other. The mineral oil might have been an improvement, but it had absorbed the acrid taint of its Bakelite lid, a taste even more nauseating than cod liver. Worse, since mineral oil is indigestible, drops of oil now dispersed on the surface of the toilet water after my bowel movements. I understood the connection between the oil I was gagging down and the oil shimmering above my stool, but I thought the phenomenon was pathological. It anguished me for weeks. Finally, on a morning when she seemed uncharacteristically sympathetic, I dared to reveal my problem. She inspected the evidence. "Oh, that's just the mineral oil," she dismissed my fears airily, but she cut my dose and eventually gave up dosing us.

I no longer wet the bed, but I needed the toilet at night. The only bathroom in the house opened directly inside her bedroom door. I used it whenever I had to, sometimes more than once a night, until she announced one day in a fury that I was getting up at night unnecessarily and disturbing her sleep.

I should make sure I relieved myself before I went to bed, she told me, because from then on I was forbidden to use the bathroom at night. "I married your *father*, not you," she added mysteriously. I understood her to mean she wanted to be alone with him at night. She meant more. "Kidneys move a good deal, gets up often during night," the social worker whom the juvenile court appointed wrote of me a year and a half later in her investigation report. "Step mother accused him of being curious to know what was going on." There was only one bathroom, and only one way to access it. If she thought I was spying on her sex life she could have supplied me with a chamber pot.

Telling someone *not* to do something to induce him to do it is a powerful form of suggestion. Dutifully I went to the bathroom just before climbing to my upper bunk on the north wall of the sleeping porch, but as soon as Stanley turned out the light and we settled down to sleep I felt my bladder fill. I lay awake then for hours. I tried to redirect my thoughts, tell myself stories, recite numbers, count sheep. I clamped my sphincters until they cramped and burned. Lying on my back, hurting and urgent, I cried silently to the ceiling low overhead, tears running down my face without consolation, only reminding me of the other flow of body fluid that my commandant had blocked. When clamping my sphincters no longer worked I pinched my penis to red pain.

Sometimes I fell asleep that way and slept through. Once or twice, early in the chronology of this torture, I wet the bed. That villainy erupted in such monstrous humiliation that I learned not to repeat it. Thereafter I added struggling to stay awake to struggling to retain my urine.

One desperate night I decided to urinate out the window. There were two windows in the porch back wall. They opened ten feet above the yard. I waited until I was sure Stanley was solidly asleep, climbed down my ladder and slipped to the nearer window. Two spring-loaded pins had to be pulled and held out simultaneously to open it. That wasn't easy to coordinate, especially since I was bent over with cramping. The window fit its frame badly. It jammed and squeaked going up. I forced it up six inches and then a foot—high enough—stood on tiptoe, my little penis barely reaching over the sill, and let go. I'd hoped the hydraulic pressure would be sufficient to drive the stream of urine through the screen, missing the ledge and the frame, but the angle was bad. I dribbled. My urine ran down the ledge and out under the screen frame. That meant it would leave a telltale stain down the outside wall. I tried forcing the stream into a higher arc and managed to pulse it in splashes through the screen. It sprayed out into the night air below a blank silver moon.

I'd barely begun when I heard noise—the bedroom door, footsteps in the dining room, the kitchen door swinging. I clamped off the flow in a panic—it was hard to stop—popped my dripping penis back into my pajamas, warm urine running down my leg, and stood at the window waiting. I prayed to God it wasn't my stepmother.

Dad stepped through the doorway, half awake. "What's going on?" he said softly.

"It was stuffy in here," I improvised. "I opened the window to get some air."

"You don't want to disturb your Aunt Anne," he told me. "Better close that thing and get back to bed."

I wasn't sure if he knew what I was doing or not. Probably not. I closed the window. He padded off. I'd managed to alleviate my urgency enough to get to sleep. To my amazement—I suppose I believed her omniscient—my stepmother only grumbled the next morning about people up at night prowling around. Even so, I knew I couldn't use the window anymore. I'd have to find some other way.

I had plenty of time at night to think. I needed a way to store my urine, an equivalent to the Schonmeier chamber pot. The top of the closet Stanley and I shared formed a deep storage shelf, level with the head of my bed. Stanley and I stashed our junk there—books, comic books, cigar boxes of crayons and pencils, homemade wooden swords. There were dozens of empty mason jars in the basement. I could bring up some jars, I worked out, urinate into them at night, hide them on the junk shelf and empty them the next day when no one was looking.

Accumulating jars was easy. I brought them up from the basement one at a time. Stanley and I used them anyway to collect fireflies and bugs and they all looked alike. Arranging them in the dark to relieve my urgent bladder was harder. Dad's and our stepmother's bed was on the other side of the wall behind the closet. We couldn't hear through the wall unless she and Dad were fighting, but I didn't dare take chances. She hadn't only forbidden me to use the bathroom at night. Because she'd offered me no alternative receptacle, she'd effectively forbidden me to urinate at night, asserting by that fiat that she, not I, controlled my bladder. Devising an alternative, as I'd done, was challenging her authority over my body. My fear of being caught reflected the risk I felt I was taking. I also had every reason to believe that if she caught me with a mason jar of urine she'd forbid me that release as well and I'd be worse off than I was before.

So I didn't open a jar to relieve myself as soon as the house quieted down. I continued my ritual of restraint, of clamping my sphincters and pinching my penis, until I could no longer bear the pain. Only then, an hour or more after bedtime, did I dare to ease a jar stealthily from its hiding place, slip it under the covers to muffle any sound and slowly unscrew its heavy zinc lid. After I'd waited a while longer to be sure no one had heard, I turned on my side, released my penis, bent it over the rough lip of the jar tilted down into the sag of my mattress and tentatively, squirting and clamping, emptied my bladder. I thought I could fill a jar and sometimes I nearly did. To avoid overflowing I pressed a finger down along the inside of the jar; when the warm urine wet it I knew I needed to stop. Hot with shame then I screwed the lid back on, struggling sometimes to start the threads straight. Then I had the concealment problem in reverse. I had to move the jar filled with urine back onto the junk shelf, and with the evidence now patent I was even more terrified of being heard. It didn't take me as long to return the jars to the shelf as it did to fetch them, but I worked tense with caution and froze every time my bunk springs squeaked.

Disposing of the jars turned out to be the hardest part. I was afraid to move them when our stepmother was home and she seldom left the house after school or during the evening. Jars of urine began accumulating on the shelf behind the junk. They didn't smell—I screwed the lids tight enough to prevent that—but the liquid turned a darker yellow and grew gray cobwebs of mold. Once in a while I had a chance to dispose of them, one or two at a time. I let Stanley in on the secret. He didn't disapprove beyond warning me of the danger. "You better hadn't let her catch you," he told me. A dozen jars collected on the shelf.

I was away all one Saturday morning doing a job, running errands or cleaning out someone's garage. When I got home

Stanley met me coming through the backyard and hissed me aside to a conference. "She almost found the jars," he whispered. I turned white. "It's okay," he said. "I got rid of them. She got mad about all the junk on the shelf and told me to clean it off. She was standing there watching me. I started cleaning stuff off but I kept moving it around to hide your jars. I got to where I didn't see how I could hide them any longer and just then the phone rang and she went off and starting jawing. I hurried up and ran the jars down the back steps and hid them out here under the old tarp. She went off after that and I came out and emptied them. Whew! they smelled bad. They smelled like dead fish." It was a close call and he wasn't happy with me for exposing him to it. After that he helped me keep them emptied.

To this day, forty years later, once a month or so, pain wakes me. Falling asleep with urine in my bladder or unmoved rectal stool, I still reflexively tighten my pelvic muscles until my sphincters cramp. My stepmother, my commandant, still intermittently controls my body even at this distant and safe remove. I sit on the toilet those nights in the silence of my house forcing my sphincters to relax, waiting out the pain in the darkness, remembering her.

4

"BASICALLY," says Stan of our stepmother, "her treatment was
to beat and to starve, and this was how you made someone
submit." Among the old photographs my brother sent me after
I visited him in Idaho was a collage of snapshots mounted on a
handmade cedar plaque. It looks like something Dad made after
he and our stepmother retired to Missouri's Lake of the Ozarks
in 1950. It's edged with green upholstery braid. An aluminum
poptop ring glued to the back makes a hanger. The snapshots,
snipped into small irregular ovals for the collage, are scratched
and torn. Two of them show Stanley and me in the Gernhardt
days, one with Dad, one with a group of children, including
Mack. Two others show Dad late in life, one behind a stone
barbecue pit he's built, one with our stepmother, the only picture
we have of her—short and fat, she's wearing a dark dress, a
pearl necklace and an elaborate hat. The other snapshot in the
collage chokes me with rage every time I look at it. It shows
Stanley and me flanking Dad in the final summer of our stepmother years. Stanley's obviously emaciated. I look like an
Auschwitz child. Our stepmother took the picture; her shadow
falls across me, as it did. When I recognized that evidence of
our abuse I searched through the rest of the collection Stan sent

me for a reference photograph. I found one, a snapshot of him and me with James Schonmeier in the summer of 1947, just before Dad and our stepmother were married. In that earlier photograph we look like healthy, normal boys. When a social worker investigated our case in July 1949, she reported that Stanley at thirteen years of age was five feet four and weighed ninety-seven pounds. My application for admission that month to the Andrew Drumm Institute notes that at twelve I was four feet eleven and weighed eighty pounds. For two years, to discipline us, to punish us and to maximize her profits from our labor, our stepmother not only beat us but also systematically starved us. Dad let it happen, protesting when he dared but too intimidated to protect us. He made his own life easier at the expense of ours. I've never forgiven him for that and never will.

The social worker's reports reveal the strategy the woman devised. Under the heading "Step Mother's Story," the report on Stanley paraphrases our tormentor: "The boys eat separately from the mother and father. Their table manners were such as they could not eat together. The father defended them. If he [i.e., one of us] wanted a second piece of pie the father said to let them have it. . . . The arguments start between the step mother and the father because of the boys." The report on me adds: "[Stepmother] make[s] children sit at a separate table, manners were so bad she could not eat at same table. Put up separate table after couple were married about six months." We can't have forgotten all the proprieties we learned at the Gernhardts', but however bad our table manners may have been, our stepmother always had the option of improving them. She certainly devoted herself to teaching us to distinguish right from left. In fact, slandering our manners gave her an excuse to remove us from the family table. Feeding us separately allowed her to starve us without argument from Dad and without having to tolerate our accusing eyes.

Our food degraded over time. I remember occasional hot dogs at first and fried baloney. Once in a while our stepmother still served us a dinner of powdered milk and warm cherry pie, the pie stale from the Manor day-old outlet store like the bread we bought. For school lunches we got one sandwich in a brown paper bag. At first she allowed us to spread the bread thinly with peanut butter before we dolloped it with a tablespoonful, no more, of the grainy, runny grape jelly she put up. Later she discontinued the peanut butter. She demanded we confine the tablespoonful of jelly to the center of the bread. When I begged to spread it to the edges to make the bread less dry she shouted me down. I didn't understand that she was begrudging us the extra measure of jelly that spreading might conceal.

Our teachers noticed the meagerness of our lunches. My fifth-grade teacher sent me to the corner grocery across from the school to buy her a half-pint of milk, always adding, "And here's a dime to buy one for yourself." She'd done the same for Stanley, supplementing our lunches out of pocket.

The ration our stepmother eventually settled on was black-eyed peas. She alternated that grim staple with hard-boiled eggs. Both were cheap and easy to prepare. As a farmer mixes animal feed, in batches, she boiled up a week's worth of black-eyed peas at a time in one pot and two weeks' worth of eggs in another. She cooked the black-eyed peas without salt or other seasoning. The eggs served for lunches, something portable to pass us in the summer and on weekends when she kicked us out of the house for the day, and if they sulfured and started to rot she forced them on us anyway. I remember at least once, late in our imprisonment, when she allowed a pot of eggs she was

129

cooking to boil dry and burn (from careless reheating the black-eyed peas were routinely burned); we ate the burned eggs, burned protein like burned hair, or went hungry. We went hungry anyway, while she and Dad dined on pork chops and even steak, the meaty sear of their frying drifting back onto the sleeping porch to tantalize us. Supper cooking made our stomachs growl; the springs of our cheeks gushed saliva.

We learned to scavenge and to steal. "I ended up eating a lot of candy," Stan remembers, "because I could get candy with just a little bit of money. In my attempt to get food, I started stealing quarters off their bureau, Dad's change. That was a big mistake, because I was caught by Auntie Anne, and Dad got in on that one. I got it good. That taught me a lesson, never to steal from them." But there was a piggy bank in the sleeping porch closet, a globe of the world, pulled partly loose from its wooden base, spilling nickels and dimes and precious quarters. It belonged to our stepmother's brother, a catchall for his pocket change that he'd left behind in storage along with some of his clothes when he moved out. Stanley stole quarters from that cornucopia to buy candy. Since the coins were no longer being replenished he had to steal parsimoniously. I stole from it too, independently and equally cautiously, specializing in dimes and nickels rather than quarters, until I discovered a less hazardous supply.

Our stepmother had a married daughter as well as a son. Rowena and her husband, Clifford, lived nearby. On Saturdays I worked for her. She was everything her mother was not—gentle, soft-spoken, compassionate. Clifford had been a navy officer during the war; they'd survived the Japanese attack on Pearl Harbor. They had a two-year-old son. I believe now that Rowena hired me in order to help me—she kept her house immaculate; there was hardly any work to do—and I've added her to my pantheon of saints. I spent months cleaning her bedroom wallpaper with wads of rubbery paste she mixed up. In love with her, dazed by her decency, I followed her around the house, eager to do her bidding. She put *Buster Brown* on the radio on Saturday morning (Buster Brown's sidekick Froggie plunking his magic twanger to transport us to a world of dramatized fairy tales), baked oatmeal cookies or cinnamon-glazed pecans and let me lick the bowls. I ground up American cheese and pimientos at her direction and she mixed them with mayonnaise to make a spread for the sandwiches she served me with fruit and potato chips and fresh lemonade for lunch. We played with the baby in a backyard splash pool, washed windows, rearranged the attic or the basement or the living room. When the baby took his nap I sat with him while she went out.

The baby had a sterling-silver piggy bank. Rowena opened it once when I was there and counted out the quarters it had swallowed, fifteen or twenty dollars in quarters and a silver dollar for each of the baby's two years. I loved Rowena and I loved her baby but I coveted his legacy of quarters reserved in their silver treasury gathering dust. The baby didn't need them. I needed them desperately. One Saturday when Rowena went out I stole a quarter from the piggy bank, the first of many, teasing it out with a table knife, crying with fear and shame. I think Rowena must have discovered my pilfering eventually. She paid me fifty cents for each Saturday's work. She knew her mother pocketed my earnings. Sometimes she gave me a quarter for myself. After I began stealing quarters from her son's piggy bank her tips stopped. She never confronted me.

Teachers' supplements and petty theft weren't enough to feed us. We scavenged as well. After school and on weekends, roaming the streets, I scouted the trash cans of drive-ins. Finding a half-eaten hamburger was rapture; I'd brush off the cigarette ashes and carry it to a nearby curb and devour it. I was hungry and it fed me. Half a bottle of warm cherry cream soda free of crickets from the drive-in trash was bliss.

One hot summer day, passing through the parking lot of the drive-in on Independence Avenue, a block from the South Quincy house, I noticed three open ten-gallon cartons of ice cream lined up on the loading dock. I vaulted up onto the dock to inspect them. One carton was nearly a third full of strawberry ice cream, the others about one-quarter full of vanilla and chocolate. I couldn't believe my eyes. Why were they sitting melting in the sun? Was it possible that the drive-in was throwing them away? One of the men who worked in the kitchen came out for a smoke and I overcame my shyness to ask him. He said the freezer had broken down. They were trashing the cartons, he said. I asked him if I could have them. He didn't see why not but he thought I ought to check with the manager. I talked to the manager through the screen door. He was doubtful. I improvised. I told him the ice cream wouldn't go to waste. I'd throw a party for all the kids in the neighborhood and tell them the ice cream was a gift from the drive-in. "Go ahead and take it," he said, "only make sure you serve it out before it goes sour."

Our stepmother was away for the day. I ran home and found Stanley and reported our incredible windfall. When he understood that there was more ice cream than we could possibly eat ourselves he warmed to the idea of a neighborhood party. Running all the way, afraid they might be gone, we raced our wagon to the drive-in and collected the three cartons.

Back home we commandeered every bowl in the house—

soup bowls, custard dishes, serving and mixing bowls—carried an old table out from the basement and set up our party on the street corner. We scouted the area for kids. We were still outsiders in that neighborhood and most of them didn't believe us at first, but they straggled along eventually to see. Some were eager. Most were nonchalant, which baffled me. From their point of view we had nothing more to offer than melting ice cream. Stanley and I thought we were offering a feast and a gift. When they'd eaten their fill, or taken a bowl and dumped it contemptuously on the sidewalk, they returned to their summer play.

We still had gallons of ice cream on hand at the end of the party. Too full to eat any more, half sick from a glut of butterfat but incapable of throwing what was left away, Stanley and I decided to freeze at least part of it. Our stepmother had made us a kind of Popsicle once by freezing Kool-Aid in an ice-cube tray. We dumped out all three of her freezer trays and filled them with melting ice cream. We were still so mortally naive that we imagined she'd be proud of us for not letting the remains of our windfall go to waste. Instead she was furious that we'd held a party in her absence without her permission, that we'd taken her bowls from the house, that we'd ruined her ice-cube trays. She threw out the ice cream and sent us to bed without supper. We didn't need it. That day at least we'd eaten our fill.

The Katz drugstore on the corner of Independence Avenue and Hardesty, two blocks east of the drive-in, had a doughnut-making machine. One bitterly cold winter Saturday when our stepmother turned us out of the house at eight in the morning with a hard-boiled egg in our pocket and ordered us not to return until six that night—if we got cold, she taunted us, maybe we'd quit being lazy and find some work to do to get warm—Stanley and I slipped into the drugstore to watch doughnuts being made. The glass-and-stainless-steel doughnut machine looked like a wide popcorn machine, but a stainless-steel dough tank was mounted where a popper would have been hung. At waist level below the dough tank a deep-fat fryer bubbled; a chain of paddles moved the doughnuts along as they fried. We stood as close as we could to this marvel. We'd have pressed our noses to the glass if it hadn't been hot. Close as we were, the warmth dispelled our shivering. I'm sure we drooled.

A valve in the bottom of the tank extruded dough. A rod extended downward and back to twirl free a white, puffy bracelet. The bracelet of dough dropped into the hot lard and immediately started sizzling, bubbles forming in the dough that burst to release a steam of yeast and egg and spice. The swelling doughnut floated along to a metal spatula mounted just below the surface of the fat. The spatula lifted the doughnut clear and flipped it over. Golden brown now on top, browning below, it floated around a corner, where the chain carried it up out of the fat onto a grillwork ramp. It bumped down the ramp, draining and cooling, and slipped off onto a work area. From there the white-uniformed woman who operated the machine sorted it plain onto a tray or iced it with chocolate, cherry, vanilla or coconut icing.

It seems to me that we watched the machine making doughnuts for at least an hour that morning. An earthquake wouldn't have dislodged me. I didn't have a penny to my name. I couldn't buy even one doughnut. It was enough simply to smell them. The steam of their frying was a cloud of manna in the air. I did begin to consider begging the solidified splashes of icing that the woman scraped to one side between batches. She didn't offer us icing. Nervously but not unkindly, she told us to go away.

We wandered to the comic-book rack. But we couldn't resist the doughnut making. Our noses led us back. We were ragamuffins with hollow eyes, and our hungry stares finally overwhelmed the woman's reserve. She wrapped four iced doughnuts in waxed paper, looked around furtively and passed them to us over the counter. I flushed with disbelief; my ears buzzed. "Here," she told us, "take these and get out of here before the manager sees me." We both said, "Thank you, ma'am," and ducked out the door into the iron cold of late morning. The doughnuts were still hot, sweet with grainy icing, heavy with lard. Nothing in all the years since that day ever filled my mouth that gave me such ecstasy, not even the soft, warm breast of a lover.

THE CITY OF Kansas City begins at the Missouri River and extends south across a series of low east-west ridges divided by creek valleys. In the modern city the runoff of rains that once made the creeks flow has been diverted underground into storm sewers, concrete pipes twelve feet in diameter that connect to the surface through drains built into the street curbs and through manholes. The storm sewers, which are separate from the pipes that carry sewage, run for miles under the city, draining into tributary rivers and eventually into the Missouri itself. In the summer of 1948 Stanley discovered the storm-sewer system and made it his own.

Summers were always better than winters in our boarding-house and stepmother years. School let out, which freed us to roam, and living on the streets was easier when it was warm. After winter days in that harsh continental climate in the twenties or thirties with nights near zero, Kansas City summers were hot and humid, the temperature in the nineties by day and high eighties by night with stretches of days peaking above one hundred degrees. Thin and hungry, we suffered from the cold but hardly noticed the heat. Summers we wandered the city like urban Huckleberry Finns.

137

By 1948 we'd both acquired bicycles, the only kind available in those days, heavy American bicycles with longhorn handlebars, fixed gears, back-pedal foot brakes and front baskets, a huge front basket in Stanley's case. Our stepmother's son organized a bicycle for Stanley from new and used spare parts. "Green bicycle," Stan remembers. "He found an old frame and helped me get going." I bought mine in one piece, used. We searched the classifieds in the *Kansas City Star* to find the cheapest wheels available and drove over to look at the most promising offer. I was horrified. It was a girl's bicycle with a V-frame to allow a skirt to clear, baby blue, and I knew I'd be ridiculed for it, called a sissy or a queer. My stepmother liked the price, however, five dollars. We bought it with my earnings, and once I learned to ride it I ignored the neighborhood jeering: it freed me to fly.

Our stepmother favored bicycle ownership because it extended our capacity to run errands and increased our earning potential. "She encouraged me to go around to the neighborhood and offer my services for cleaning and hauling away stuff," Stan says. "It didn't amount to a whole lot. I couldn't get a whole lot of trash on my big basket." He needed a place to dump the trash. We had a place. We called it the swamp.

There's a raft in this story. Near the corner of Independence Avenue and Hardesty, on east from the Katz drugstore, the U.S. Army maintained a massive gray concrete warehouse surrounded by high Cyclone fencing. During the war, so I understood, it had served for graves registration, collecting the bodies of soldiers killed in battle and processing their effects before shipping them home. That made it a vast temporary mausoleum, and I never passed it without feeling the dark energies it radiated, energies of adulthood with all its bewildering freedom and violence and loss, the same dark energies I felt at my mother's grave (we never visited my mother's grave anymore; I'm sure our stepmother was jealous of her even dead, as she was furiously jealous of Gretta Schonmeier, as certain as Mr. Schonmeier had been that Dad had slept with her). Beyond the graves registration building eastward was a swamp, an area of bad drainage backed up from a tributary creek at the eastern edge of the city.

"Big old lakey swamp," Stan recalls. "It's probably gone. We used to build—I'd built, I don't remember how much you were involved—a raft, and we'd pole out on the raft like Huck Finn and Tom Sawyer. At some point I'd explored this whole area, because we had days and days where we had nothing to do. We were kicked out, okay? Nobody cared about this area. That's why I dumped trash there.

"Out of one end of the swamp came this huge pipe"—one of the storm sewers—"and up from it came this manhole. The manhole was sticking out of the ground a few feet. When you took the lid off, the rebars were built right into the manhole to make a ladder, so you could climb way down, belowground. That's how I discovered the tunnels. First I dropped stones into it, then I went down, looked around and came back up. Each time I went farther along. It had connections. It was like the sewers of Paris."

Stanley took over the sewers that summer. He lit his way with his Boy Scout flashlight. He wandered for miles, emerging at the corners of major intersections to peer out at the world through the drain gratings. He even popped up in the middle of streets, cautiously tipping up a manhole cover, ducking and clanging it back down a beat ahead of the wheels of approaching cars. "I had an old BB gun. I took that down there for protection, to shoot the rats." He was lucky enough not to be caught underground when it rained and the sewers flooded with runoff. Rain refreshed them, cleaned the rotting vegetation out.

He tried once to give me a tour. "We saved money and got this unusual flashlight that strapped onto our wrist. That's when I took you down there, because I thought, Oh, he won't be afraid with this wonderful flashlight." I was more than afraid. I was terrified. All I could think of was rats. Ten feet along from the manhole where we entered I started screaming. Unimpressed with my claustrophobia, Stanley threatened to walk away and leave me to find my way out on my own. I begged him not to abandon me. When it was clear that I was panicked beyond calming he relented. He led me back to the rebar ladder and saw me safely up. I looked down from the world of light to his pale, upturned face. He waved his flashlight solemnly, like a conductor signaling the departure of a train, and trudged off into the darkness. I never went back into one of his tunnels, nor ever wanted to.

I don't know if he'd read *Les Misérables* by then and imagined himself Jean Valjean. He may have, or maybe we saw the movie. He'd found a place where he felt safe. "Because I was a boy trying to get away into my own world, and this horrible, dark, filthy world was a world where no one else would go, and I was free in this world. I could fantasize this to a huge fantasy." Could and did, to escape the darker and more horrible emotional world to which necessity chained us. We always went home at night. Where else was there to go?

I missed Stanley that summer. He disappeared for whole days, returning home at dark to lie away his whereabouts, eat a plate of black-eyed peas and sleep, disappearing again early the next morning. With a bicycle I wasn't as lonely as I might have been. I roamed the entire northeastern quarter of the city on my bike, coasting its long hills cool in the breeze of passage. I watched streetcars and electric buses coming and going from a big trolley barn mazed with overhead lines and tracks, a domesticated version of Dad's vulcan roundhouse. Nearby there was a lumberyard redolent of oak and pine that I could explore, wondering at all the varied cuts of molding and lath and board, attracted to the smell of creosoted posts like the creosoted railroad ties of my summer in Utica with the Schonmeiers. The swamp had trees to climb and vines I tested like Tarzan. Limestone fountains in the city parks bubbled cool water to drink and there were tall chain swings with smooth oak seats where I swung for an hour at a time, pumping myself high above the ground and jumping off into the next county. I could always scout grocery-store and drive-in trash barrels for lunch if my hard-boiled egg was spoiled. Three pop bottles returned for the deposit still bought a Baby Ruth bar, with a penny left over for bubble gum. Everywhere I bicycled I stopped to watch people going about their lives, families in particular, fascinated with their quaint and alien normality. Numbed, adapted to such extremity that I was hardly even jealous, I felt like a man from Mars.

Most of all I read. If Stanley escaped into his tunnels, I escaped into books. Not exactly books in those years. Pulp science fiction. I don't remember when I discovered those thick, journal-sized anthologies of extragalactic melodrama. They were printed on coarse newsprint and perfect-bound between lurid four-color covers. Each issue offered several hundred smeared pages of tales of futuristic cops and robbers, cowboys and Indians, heroes and bug-eyed monsters and damsels in distress. They cost a quarter. That was how I spent the quarters I stole from Rowena's baby, not for food but for pulp science fiction, the next rung up from comic books. I went through one a week and could have gone through two or three if I'd had the money to buy them. Sometimes, shaking with hunger but with only a quarter to spend, I wept tears of frustration at having to choose between buying food and buying a pulp. Even hungry I more often chose the pulp. I could stanch my hunger with black-eyed peas. The pulps fed my soul. I escaped through them into a world that had shape, a world where underdogs triumphed, a world where even the most cunning and malevolent monsters were always outwitted in the end and destroyed.

I found consolation in the pulps beyond their escapist stories. Along their back pages a sideshow of advertising promised redemption through self-help: Charles Atlas muscle building, correspondence schools that taught car mechanics and commercial art and radio repair, acne creams, trusses, foreign pen pals (I corresponded for a time with a girl my age in Scotland), odd religions symbolized by cyclopean eyes set in obelisks beaming rays of holy light. Like Gatsby I believed their promises, sent off for their free literature, fantasized that personal discipline and secret revelations might improve my lot. Stanley and I seldom went to church. When we did, ragged starvelings that we were, indictments of middle-class complacency, we were pointedly ignored. Charles Atlas welcomed ninety-eight-pound weaklings; the Rosicrucians had the secrets of the ages to share. I needed hope to sustain me: pulps and their promises were the best I could cobble together at the time.

By then I had nightmares. Three of them recurred, so vividly I always woke from them shaking with terror and had to struggle even awake to break free. One began ballistically: I was arcing high into the air over my grade school as if I'd been fired from a cannon. Then, sickeningly, I began to fall. I could

142

see the playground coming up below me and the sidewalk wall. I always woke before I hit.

The second nightmare opened on a drive in the country, a recreation the Rhodes family sometimes pursued on Sundays, as if our scavenging excursions weren't enough. ("Step mother said they used to go on rides on Sunday afternoons," the social worker reports, "and she was of the opinion that they should sit in the back seat and have a conversation and then when the car was stopped they could run and yell. The boys did not do this. They talked and jabbered and scuffeled [sic] with one another. She said they even kissed each other [once, making fun of romantic love—what a dirty mind the woman had]. She has stopped all the Sunday rides with them and told the father to take them. The boys go alone now on Sundays." That ought to have been a relief, but I still got carsick.) Driving in the country in my nightmare, we stopped at a pretty roadside creek. I walked over to drink from it and stepped off a bluff and began falling. It wasn't a roadside creek. It was a river, its scale diminished by distance, deadly, running far below.

The third nightmare was the worst of the three by far. Near one of the schools we'd attended we'd crossed a major intersection through an underpass. In my nightmare I descended into that underpass only to find myself lost in a tunnel—not one of Stanley's tunnels, which he hadn't discovered when this recurrent dream began, but a variant of the tunnel of malevolent trees in the movie *Snow White and the Seven Dwarfs*. The tunnel walls widened at waist height to ledges punctuated with dark holes, and out of those holes gnarled hands with long, vicious claws writhed up to snatch at me as I passed. I saw light at the end of the tunnel and began to hope that arriving there might put me beyond the reach of danger. I ran desperately, my legs hardly working, forcing myself forward to safety, but coming out of the darkness, too late to turn around, I saw that ahead was a dead end, another and wider ledge, a larger hole, and a black-cloaked witch, her face the contorted face of my stepmother, screeched up from the hole and arched over fiendishly to grab me.

We had our tonsils out that year at Children's Mercy Hospital, Stanley in one bed and I in the next, another kind of abuse. No one told us what was happening; I arrived on the operating room table dizzy with sedative and unprepared. I panicked when the anesthetist set a gauze cone over my nose and mouth and began dripping ether. I couldn't breathe. I started screaming and fought to climb off the table. Strangers in masks held me down until I passed out. I dreamed my head was lodged at the bottom of a black whirlpool, my body swirling away at the top in a rainbow-colored sea, and woke to sick nausea and the sight of Stanley retching clots of black blood into a kidney basin. Back home I filled a glass with saliva rather than brave the sharp pain of swallowing. Our stepmother looked in from the kitchen from time to time to ridicule our misery. Curled up fetally, licking my wounds, I wanted to stay in bed forever. We came home on a Friday. Monday she sent us back outdoors to fend for ourselves.

By the summer of 1948 we'd taken up smoking. We weren't trying to be tough. Nicotine curbed our hunger. Cigarettes were hard to get. They weren't sold in vending machines then and sales to minors over the counter were illegal. We picked butts from the sidewalk and sometimes got our hands on a pack. "We smoked Dominos," says Stan. "Really horrible brand of cigarette. Sometimes Pall Mall. We never smoked that much because we never accumulated enough to do it." I don't think we dared to steal from Dad.

Behind a stretch of old storefronts and repair shops along one of the streets that paralleled Independence Avenue to the south, a creek bent around an open back lot. The lot was overgrown with weeds and partly shaded by the trees that lined the creek. On one of our expeditions Stanley and I noticed a ten-foot wooden camping trailer installed on concrete blocks at the edge of the creek bank. The door hung open. If no one lived there it might make a hideout. We sauntered up to see and smelled pipe tobacco.

There was a woman inside, sitting on a kitchen chair smoking a cigarette. She came into the doorway to greet us. She was about the same age and build as our stepmother, but she welcomed us warmly and she was easy to talk to.

She told us to stop back anytime and we did. We started hanging out with her. Stanley came and went from his tunnels. I arrived first thing in the morning and had to be asked to leave. Across the summer I learned her story. She and her husband had been itinerant photographers. The trailer had been their studio and their home. Her husband had run off, local studios had come along, the photography business had dried up and the trailer beside the creek was all she had left. Her son sent her a little money to live on. We called her the gypsy lady.

The gypsy lady found out the Fourth of July was my birthday and promised she'd bake me a cake. I didn't see how she could bake a cake when she only had a hot plate but she promised me she would. I turned up early on my birthday—evil little troublemaker that I was, we weren't celebrating it at home— and found her mixing the cake in a glass bowl. She set the bowl in a pan of water and inverted a larger mixing bowl over the pan. The cake cooked for an hour, breathing cinnamon and clove, and came out gray, steamed to a pudding rather than baked. I ate at least half the pudding cake on my own. The gypsy lady happily watched me eat it and took a small piece herself. Stanley showed up to polish off the rest.

The gypsy lady rolled her own cigarettes with pipe tobacco. That was why they smelled the way they did. She used a rolling machine, a red rubber belt fitted onto a metal frame the size of a pencil sharpener. In its open position the belt formed a U that accepted a cigarette paper. The gypsy lady sprinkled a line of Prince Albert pipe tobacco from a red-enameled hip-pocket tin across the bottom of the U, levered the belt back and forth and ejected a perfectly formed cigarette ready to lick and glue.

She shared her aromatic cigarettes. She rolled three instead of one and we sat on her wooden stoop puffing away, a lonely woman and two dusty summer boys.

She was nearly as poor as we. We concocted schemes to help her or at least pay our share. "We were always trying to hustle for the gypsy lady," Stan says. "We sold puppies for her one time." I didn't remember that she had a dog. I loved dogs. "Yeah. And she let us keep some of the money. We bought or she gave us a pack of cigarettes for it."

"Didn't there come a time when she felt guilty for supplying us with tobacco and cigarettes?"

"No, there came a time when Granny Annie found out. She went down with Dad and they chewed the gypsy lady out royally. So the gypsy lady felt that we'd betrayed her. I went back to see her about a week later and she told me to get off the property. We *had* sort of finked on her. We couldn't help it. It was under duress. Maybe they'd caught us with a cigarette." End of the gypsy lady.

We revenged the tonsillectomies. For some reason our step-mother took a tuberculin test. It turned up positive. We were tested regularly in school, two pricks on the forearm to observe for swelling. I always tested positive, which meant I'd once been infected, but the disease wasn't active, as a subsequent X ray at a mobile X-ray unit that parked outside the school always confirmed. Her X ray must have been ambiguous. Tuberculosis was still a widespread and serious disease in the United States in 1948. For a definitive workup our stepmother had to go to the Leeds Sanitarium, east of our neighborhood above the industrial district on a hill. She packed in a rage, tearfully, ranting, throwing things, stamping her feet. I was to blame. I was the carrier. I'd brought tuberculosis into her house. I'd picked it up from the old man who used to live upstairs (I remember the accusation, but not the old man). Dad delivered her to the sanitarium. The house was quiet and we were glad. "I hope she dies," Stanley cursed her. I told him he wasn't supposed to say that. I was afraid she would hear or God would. "I don't care," Stanley repeated. "I hope she dies." Secretly I hoped so too.

She returned two days later to wait for the results of the test. We overheard her say that the procedure had been horrible, that they'd tried repeatedly to force a tube down her nose into her stomach while she fought them and that they'd finally let her go to sleep and caught her off guard in the middle of the night and had their way with her. We were glad to hear she'd been violated. It was July or August by then, hot summer, and imagining herself mortally ill, playing Camille, she moved to a bed Dad set up for her on the front porch and spread her dark, wavy hair across a white pillow. Dad sat beside her in the evening darkness while we hung around the front yard. They talked quietly and she wept. His cigarette glowed and darkened for her as it once had done for me.

Eventually Dad came to the screen door and called us to

the porch. "Your Aunt Anne has something she wants to tell you," he explained. We shuffled up for inspection and stood above her, looking down at her face swollen with crying. Without her makeup she looked ugly and old.

"I know you boys think of me as a mean old stepmother," she began, self-pity softening her voice. "I know you don't like all the rules we have around here. Well, I've got tuberculosis now and I think I'm going to die. I just want you to know that whatever mean things you've thought about me, I've always loved you boys." I stiffened at the lie. "I've tried to take care of you the best way I know how." She started crying. "You may not have loved me," she told us, catching her breath, "but I'm going to die and you should forget all the bad things you think about me and start loving me now. You've been mean to me, you talk about me behind my back, but I forgive you for that now because I think you're good boys underneath. I want you to kneel down here by my bed and say a prayer to God to forgive you for your thoughts and help you to love your mother." Stanley and I looked at each other in horror and her eyes flashed. "I *am* your mother. Your real mother's been dead a long time. I'm the only mother you've got now." Stanley was being stubborn. He wasn't moving to kneel. I wanted to stand by him but I couldn't hold out long. Even dying she was dangerous.

Dad said, "Go on, boys, do like she says."

What choice was there? I knelt. Stanley glared at me. But it was three against one. He slipped to his knees.

"Now you repeat after me," our stepmother told us. "Dear God, I'm sorry for the bad things I have thought about my Aunt Anne."

"Dear God," we mumbled, "I'm sorry for the bad things I have thought about my Aunt Anne."

"I know she loves us very much and we'll be very sad if she dies."

"I know she loves us very much"—I was choking—"and we'll be very sad if she dies"—and then I had to fight to avoid giggling.

"And I will try to love her now and ever after and remember her always."

"And I will try to love her now and ever after and remember her always."

"Now tell me that you love me," she finished. I did, nearly gagging, and gave her the hug she held out her flabby arms to demand. Stanley didn't budge until Dad pinched him.

The tests were negative. She didn't die. She wasn't even ill. But she'd seen our glee at her misfortune and understood we'd wished her dead. After that she redoubled her brutality. Our final year with her was all-out war, a war we almost lost.

6

IT WASN'T THAT we were desperately poor. Our stepmother was saving to start a dress shop. That's where the money went that she stole from us and the money she saved by starving us. Sometime that fall we moved to a storefront at 3505 East Ninth Street, about a mile and a half southwest of South Quincy and our school. The social worker evaluates the Ninth Street quarters generously in her report: "Store room in front, nice cooking, power machine, hem stitch machine, small sewing machine, all electric appliances, living quarters better than average." The social worker must have been enamored of sewing machines and accustomed to a wretched average. The "store room" was the dress shop, behind a plate-glass window, where our stepmother did alterations, custom-made an occasional dress and sold her sewing and crocheting and an assortment of notions. A curtain draped across the back of the public area divided off our dark, constricted new home: hers and Dad's double bed against the west wall, a washing machine, a wash sink next where Dad shaved in the morning, a toilet in the corner enclosed in a dark green closet of painted tongue-and-groove pine with a creaky door, a table and chairs along the back wall, the doorway to our room, a refrigerator and stove and kitchen sink against the

east wall. Dad's armchair and her rocker took up the little space
left in the center. They usually passed the evening at the table
in any case, kitchen-table-style, smoking and arguing or listening to the radio.

The door to our room was a heavy meat-locker door that
our stepmother didn't allow us to close, the better to monitor
our betrayals. Attached onto the back of the building like a
shed, the unheated room we moved into that fall was only six
feet wide and nine feet long; our bunks, jammed against the
west wall, barely fit the space. The room had one window with
the glass papered over and an outside door. We shared one desk
for schoolwork. That was where we ate, one of us, the other
sitting on the lower bunk. "Now boys eat in their bed room,"
the social worker corroborates, adding from my testimony,
"Often food is mouldy, [stepmother] never buys fruit." For us,
that is. There was fruit on the table in plenty for her and Dad.

Storing our clothes in our cell of a room wasn't a problem:
we hardly owned any. Our stepmother applied some of the money
we earned to buying our clothes, but since she had other uses
for our earnings, she allowed us to buy only a bare minimum
and expected us to wear our purchases until they ripped and
rotted beyond repair, not that she repaired them. She took us
to buy our clothes to a wholesale dry-goods outlet in an old
warehouse near the river in downtown Kansas City, showing her
merchant's license to get in. To forestall argument and minimize
expense she picked out our wardrobe: striped T-shirts—long-
or short-sleeved depending on the season—bib overalls, knit
cotton undershorts, cotton socks, high-topped black basketball
shoes. For winter we bought workmen's winter coats—blue
denim coats lined with coarse wool—and thin brown cotton work
gloves. I hated my clothes because they set me apart from

everyone else at school. So did our infrequent haircuts, boot-camp crew cuts that grew out to fright wigs. As our clothes fell into disrepair and we emerged looped and ragged from that shop crowded with sewing machines I worried less about fashion and more about the gaping seams in the shoulders of my T-shirts, the ripped buttonholes that allowed the sides of my bib overalls to unfurl and expose my dirty undershorts, the back pockets that hung flapping off my bony backside, the holes in my frayed canvas shoes that let in the rain and snow, the grit and fetor of my stiff, foul socks. "I can remember we were in rags, practically," says Stan. "My tennis shoes were always a shambles. I ran around without socks on half the time."

Stan swerves: "Do you remember the bottle-of-urine incident?"

"A particular incident?"

"At the dress shop location," he explains.

I'm shocked. I didn't remember that the toilet continued off-limits at night after we moved, but I immediately understand that it must have, since I'd have had to cross through their sleeping area to use it, just as before.

"You had to pee at night," Stan reminds me. "You got spanked for it a whole bunch of times. We had double bunk beds. You slept on top and I slept down below. So we developed a technique where you would do it up there and hand it down to me." We must have adopted that arrangement after the move to the dress shop, where I had no shelf on which to hide my humiliating jars. "You would slip me a bottle of urine and I would get it back under the bed and then when I got up in the morning—I was usually the first one to get up—I'd grab that bottle and since, you know, it was time to get up anyway, I would tiptoe into the bathroom and urinate, and then pour your

153

urine out of there, rinse it and everything all in one shot and then tiptoe back and hide the bottle for the next time.

"One day Dad caught me in the act. I was holding the bottle behind my back and he said, 'What are you doing?' I said—real quietly because she was still in bed—'I'm emptying a bottle of pee.' And he said, 'Well, why?' I said, 'Because we get spanked if we get up at nighttime to pee.' Because it woke her up or whatever. And he just looked and looked, and I could see tears welling up in his eyes. I know he spoke to her about that and they had an argument about it. But I don't think anything changed."

From morning to morning my brother risked a severe beating to dump my urine for me. "That was horrible," he says, meaning denying a child the toilet. "Gee, that was really horrible. That was something you can never forgive her for." I haven't, and I won't, but suffering is never meaningless. The memory of the woman's malice will always return to me now with its complement, knowledge of my brother's courage in risking himself to help me, and gratitude for it and love.

I went back to my old neighborhood this year to look around. The storefront at 3505 East Ninth was still there, hardly changed except that painted plywood replaced the big plate-glass window. The one toilet still held court in the closet in the corner. The toilet door still creaked. The back room was as narrow and dark and cold as ever, a cell meant for punishment with a cracked and heaved raw concrete floor, but it serves only for storage now. Irony still filigrees the edges of the opaque world to admit a little light, and 3505 East Ninth Street today is a private day-care center. I told the woman who answered the door that I'd lived there once, unimaginably long years ago. She was kind enough to let me look around. That was when I saw the toilet. Public and private areas were no longer separated. Low tables crowded with children filled the long room, voices cascading like snow water or a reunion of angels, and children's paintings constellated the bright walls. While I was inspecting the back room, two little guys sidled up to me hungry for attention. They might have been Stanley and I; I kidded them, tousled their hair and traded big smiles. I stumbled out of that place of transmuted monstrosity with tears in my eyes, walked back to my rented car, stared out the windshield until I could speak again, took my tape recorder and dictated, "Oh Stan, it was so small in there, there was hardly any room at all." The back room, I meant. It was narrower than I'd remembered, narrow enough to choke me. In *The Body in Pain*, Elaine Scarry speaks of "the prisoner's steadily shrinking ground that wins for the torturer his swelling sense of territory." For two years our stepmother funneled us into smaller and smaller spaces of physical and mental confinement—less food, less room, less nurture, less hope—in order to swell her own. In time, under her vicious regimen, we might have come to occupy no space at all.

Not yet strong enough to revolt, we tried to compensate by ballooning out to fill the universe. Stanley expanded underground through his grandiose network of tunnels. I inflated myself in flights of megalomaniacal fantasy. Asked in school to write an essay about what we would wish if we had three wishes, I wished that children everywhere might be properly fed and clothed and loved, that the world might be at peace and that all the animals might be removed to a secret island where humans could no longer find them to cause them harm. I felt sweet and dreamy writing it; it made my teacher cry.

When we adopted trees in school I adopted the ailanthus, the tree of heaven, a pollution-tolerant exotic imported from

Asia that has become a weed of city alleys and vacant lots, a trash tree with an unpleasant odor that spreads noxiously underground. I cherished that ugly tree, learned that its milky sap has commercial potential as a source of rubber and made its story a parable, the Despised Tree of Unrecognized Virtue. I even called a local tire manufacturer and talked a salesman into donating a piece of uncured latex to the display I was assembling, but my stepmother refused to drive me to the factory to pick it up.

Schoolwork had always been easy for me. I almost always finished my work ahead of my classmates. My teachers usually allowed me to fill my spare time with reading. That arrangement continued in the sixth grade, after the move to East Ninth Street, but instead of library books I began reading my pulps in class, slipping a pulp from under my desktop into my workbook and departing the planet. The teacher, who'd been Stanley's the year before, usually overlooked my illicit reading, but once, inexplicably, she snatched up the pulp I was hiding, waved it over her head and announced to the class angrily that it was trash.

"It isn't trash!" I shouted back. She threatened to confiscate it and I screamed at her that it was mine. She hauled me out into the hall then. She'd been my ally; I couldn't understand why she'd turned on me. "You love Stanley more than you love me!" I accused her, and broke down sobbing. She caught herself, softened her voice, gathered me in. She loved me just as much as she loved my brother, she told me once I'd calmed, but she wasn't having trashy magazines in her classroom. If I wanted to read then I could go to the bookshelf and find something worthwhile.

I was too disturbed to read her books. The totality of violence and deprivation in my life demanded melodramatic compensation on a galactic scale. Denied my pulps, I ballooned on outward, my boundaries thinning as I stretched. I began filling the pages of my Big Chief tablets with drawings of a rocket, one rocket, one ideal rocket per page, an old-fashioned rocket in the Buck Rogers mode, maternal, with vanes like skirts, wings like arms, pregnant with a cockpit, head ablated to a point. I can draw it still, exactly as I drew it then over and over again.

Obsessed with my escapist vision, dazed, I had to tear myself away to do my schoolwork. I was the pilot, the tiny figure in the cockpit. I truly and seriously believed that if I got the drawing right—the curves of body and fins perfectly matched, the proportions balanced, the cockpit just so—my rocket would materialize with me inside it and I would roar away to freedom. I never got it right. That's why I drew it repetitively. Something was always wrong with it. If I'd drawn it right and it hadn't materialized I'd have been mired that much more hopelessly.

The storefront on East Ninth Street that the social worker judged better than average had no bathtub. Dad and our stepmother bathed regularly in a zinc washtub (privacy for bathing, which she did at leisure, was one reason she gave for kicking us outdoors). But she had more important things to do than filling bathtubs for ingrate boys. Dad, who once had taken us in his strong hands and bathed us, didn't notice or didn't dare. Officially we were allowed to wash ourselves at the wash sink, but a mess at the sink was an inconvenience that interrupted her day or ruined her evening. Between us and the sink, as between me and the toilet, she installed a minefield of threatened violence. Stanley and I went dirty. My brother started taking surreptitious sponge baths when she was occupied in the front of the store on the phone or with a customer. I was too afraid. We had tub baths that last year no more than once a month. Of

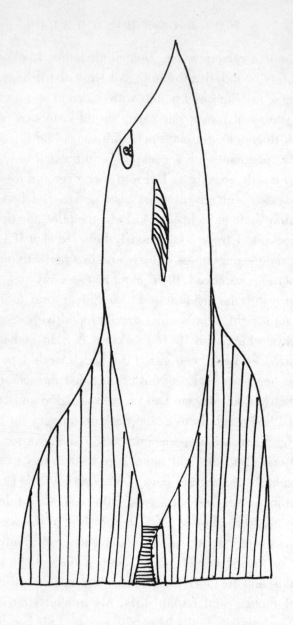

all her sadistic deprivations, even starving us, I despise her
most for forcing us to live in filth. The dirt on my body disrupted
not only my bodily integrity but also my fragile connection with
other human beings, my classmates and my teachers. My ears
were black. My neck was black. My armpits and my groin were
black. My socks rotted off my feet. I stank.

"We were dirty," Stan says quietly, his voice thinning with
suppressed rage. "Grubby boys. We couldn't be bathed. I had
a teacher named MacFarland. She was very, very kind to us. I
think that got me through a lot of bad stuff. I can remember her
straightening my shirt and trying to make me presentable. She
would find ways to clean me up. She'd take a washcloth and go
over my head." He imitates her lilt. " 'You have such pretty
hair, I just love . . .' She didn't love my hair at all. She wanted
to clean it. She was pretending to stroke my hair while she
cleaned me up."

I had a friend—I thought he was a friend—another red-
headed kid, who sat immediately behind me in school. I passed
him rocket drawings sometimes, notes, even stories torn out of
my pulps when I was still getting away with reading them. We
whispered together. I told him about the crush I had on a pretty,
dark-haired girl who sat three rows farther back.

We played dodgeball at recess. Dodgeball was my sport.
I was light and quick and often managed to escape being picked
off until I was the last of my team inside the circle, the winner
of the round. My friend was usually my competition. One day
I kidded him too sharply when he lost and I won. He gathered
a knot of classmates afterward, the girl I dreamed about among
them. They strolled over and surrounded me. They were smiling
and I thought they were friendly; it didn't occur to me to dodge.
The boys grabbed me. My friend led them. "You stink," he told

me happily. "We think you're dirty. We want to see." They jerked down the straps on my bib overalls, held my arms high, peeled off my ragged shirt. They exposed my filth, my black armpits, my dirty neck, for everyone to see. The faces of those children, the girl well forward among them, filled with horror perverted with glee. I went the only way I could go, down, dropping to the asphalt of the playground. They formed a circle around me, laughing and pointing. I couldn't get away. I covered my head and drew up my knees. I knew how to make myself invisible. I'd learned to make myself invisible when my stepmother attacked. It worked because I couldn't see her even if she could still see me. I made myself invisible. They couldn't hear me crying.

After a while they lost interest in the invisible thing I had become on the ground. They stopped jeering and drifted away. I got up and pulled my shirt back on. I thought my legs might not work, I thought a tunnel might open with ledges of searching claws, but they worked well enough. Human beings are tough. They take a lot of killing. I walked off the playground before the end of recess and went back inside and sat at my desk. I began drawing a rocket. I kept my head down when the others came in. I didn't play dodgeball after that. I stayed in at recess and read unless the teacher made me go out. "A lot of pride," the social worker writes, unrecognizably, of the child I was then, "likes to be indoors most of all. Rather read than play ball and other sports."

CHAPTER

7

THE END CAME none too soon. I don't know what I would
have ripened to if our ordeal had continued, but evidently I was
on the edge of psychosis. When, years afterward, I sat down
with a contract in hand to write my first novel and second book,
another bare fiction burst out ahead of it unbidden, a novel of
137 furious pages that I wrote in one white-hot week. *Assassin*
constructs the childhood of a psychotic named Billy who pre-
pares to assassinate a president, and many of the incidents I've
described here appear in that *cri de coeur* disguised among other
incidents I made up. "He took up the rifle and rested the barrel
on the empty window frame," the sinister little novel concludes,

> and then the limousine was coming out from under the window and
> it moved slowly on down the street and he shouldered the rifle and
> looked through the scope and there was the President and he centered
> the head in his scope and then he squeezed off a round for himself
> and then he squeezed off a round for [his hallucinated animal com-
> panion] Felean and then he squeezed off the last round for all the
> dead and murdered children of all the thousands of years of the
> world and the handsome young head exploded

Coming out of college I'd been drawn intensely to John
Kennedy, I'd taken his nomination personally, the night of his

161

nomination I'd dreamed that he and his father stood on the Capitol steps congratulating *me*—one of the many dreams of famous people I produced in my twenties and thirties to mingle with achievement and try it on for size. But when Kennedy was assassinated and I learned what maimed soul had murdered him I felt acutely that Lee Harvey Oswald might have been me. Below and behind the dreams of glory I had that much rage fused and tamped in, almost that much, as *Assassin* makes clear. Really the rage fueled the ambition, which sounds like a formula for shaping the shock wave into something useful, and it has been, but so did Oswald's. The difference is that I had help along the way—from the Gernhardts, from teachers, from the gypsy lady, from Stanley most of all—help and love. Because of Stanley's help and love in particular I got out in time. Stanley saved us. Without question he risked his life.

In Stan's recollection as in mine, the storefront days on East Ninth Street were the darkest time of all. "We were pushed out more. The food became much worse. The food became horrible. I remember the eggs, some that were let go so long that they were spoiled and tasted horribly like old sulfur. The bread was second-day. It was almost moldy to begin with. I would always supplement as much as I could with candy. But it was the increasing amount of chores, too. And farming me out to strange ladies to clean and haul away stuff and just labor after labor." One of the labors I deeply resented was making crepe-paper roses to sell. I'd learned the craft at a neighborhood community center, one of my few forays out into the world, and brought a bouquet home to our stepmother as a surprise. With derision for my gesture she commended my initiative, set me to hours of monotonous piecework at home after school and added crepe-paper roses to our inventory door-to-door.

162

Stanley had completely suppressed the memory of our mother's suicide. Viciously one day, a further violation, our stepmother informed us. Stanley mentioned the incident to the social worker: "The boy tells that he did not know his real mother committed suicide until his step mother told him." When I went out to Idaho I hadn't yet seen the investigation reports, nor had Stan. Neither of us realized, even all these years later, that he was the one who'd discovered our mother dead in the bathroom after she'd shot herself. In Idaho he remembered the incident as he'd reported it to the social worker forty years before. "At some point when Granny Annie blew up at us and was really giving us verbal abuse as well as the other, she said, 'No wonder your mother shot herself.' And that was the first time we ever knew that our mother had killed herself. Previous to that we'd always thought our mother had got sick and died in a hospital— that she had, you know, health problems or something. Dad was always very vague about that. He immediately said, 'You shouldn't have said that. You shouldn't have told them. They don't need to know that. They've never known that.' So then they hushed it up, but I asked her the next day and she said, 'Yes, your mother shot herself.' I asked more about it but she wouldn't tell me any more. So then I thought about that and thought about that and thought about that, and I went down to see this lady at the Katz drugstore who was Dad's brother's ex-wife. I said, 'Is this true?' She said, 'Yes.' So I went off and cried and cried and cried." He confronted Dad again. "I got nothing but a mumbling. You know, something like, 'Well, you shouldn't know about that. Don't ask about it. I can't tell you about that.' "

Stan dates the beginnings of our rebellion from this time, the spring and early summer of 1949, when he was thirteen and a half and I was turning twelve. "One of the things that was happening to us at the storefront was that we were breaking away from her. Bicycles gave us a lot of freedom. She could sense she had less control over us. 'They're starting to rise up and they want a portion of their earnings and they want *food!*' And we *were* rebelling. We weren't living up to her expectations. We wanted more food. We wanted to be clothed."

Our stepmother apparently decided to get rid of us. "The step mother took them to the welfare department two weeks ago," the social worker reported on July 23. Before that, she and Dad hauled us to the Andrew Drumm Institute—a private boys' home on a 360-acre working farm southeast of Independence, Missouri—to see if Drumm would take us. The superintendent, Harry Nelson, a short-legged, barrel-chested man with a leonine head of silver hair, a shrewd and tough former schoolteacher and dairy farmer, talked to them while some of the boys gave us a tour. In those days Drumm only accepted orphans and boys from broken homes, so we weren't eligible in any case, but something happened between Mr. Nelson and our stepmother as well. "At some point," says Stan, "he told her to go. The guy was sharp. He saw right through her, I'm sure." I remember the visit because she and Dad had a violent argument on the drive home about her encounter with Mr. Nelson. At its full fury, while the car was moving with traffic between stoplights, she flung open her door and threatened to jump out. Dad braked the car but hadn't stopped completely when she jumped, Stanley and I wide-eyed at the window. There were cars moving ahead and behind us and Dad had to go on. Shifting to the rear window, we glimpsed our stepmother on the sidewalk brushing herself off and then we were gone. Dad circled the block anxiously and found her striding down the sidewalk in full wrath.

He pulled to the curb and coasted along beside her, begging her to get in. Eventually she did. As soon as she shut the door she fired a new round—"You son of a bitch, you drove off and left me!"

She must have felt afflicted that summer, with two boys who stole food from her kitchen and disappeared into the hot day, eleemosynary institutions that refused to follow orders and Dad probably resisting having his sons dumped. "Instead of drinking water," the social worker paraphrases her, "they go to the ice box and drink milk instead. They take milk, marshmallows and cookies out of the home. She says the father spoils them and shields them. . . . The arguments start between the step mother and the father because of the boys. Father says things to the step mother that are terrible for the children to hear. Step mother feels that whatever she says doesn't mean anything to them. In fact, Stanley will tell her that." Dad was rebelling too. Once when she ordered him to whip us he made sure she couldn't see into our room from where she was sitting, gestured to us to pretend to cry and smacked his hand instead of our backsides with his belt. Intrepid improvisation, but if he meant the subterfuge to relieve us, it failed. It disheartened us; it demonstrated that her tyranny even intimidated a grown man. *
Faced with our tentative gestures of rebellion, she conceived a draconian further punishment that summer. "Children are not permitted to listen to the radio, read, after six months if they behave they can have it." For long evenings we sat in silence and semidarkness in our squalid back room, staring at the wall. Books were my hideout and I loved to read: six months was a life sentence.

*A friend suggests I explain somewhere along here why Stanley and I never confronted Dad, never demanded our rights. Does it need explaining? What rights?

A fight between our stepmother and Dad one day that summer came to blows, another escalation. The temperature had
pushed above one hundred degrees that day and Dad had arrived
home exhausted. She started in on him the minute he walked
in the door and I think he gestured to swat her. She whipped
off one of her stiletto shoes and cracked him in the head with
it. His eyelids fluttered and he collapsed to the floor like a
slackened puppet. I stood watching this savagery. It looked as
if she'd knocked him out. She jeered that he was faking. She
kicked at him a few times to taunt him, kicked at his head,
which made me whimper and twitch in sympathy. That brought
me to her attention. She clicked to the refrigerator, extracted a
full pitcher of ice water, clicked to me and put it in my hands
and told me to douse him with it. "That'll show who's play-
acting," she said. I was afraid to disobey her, but I was also
afraid the shock would kill him. The conflict froze me where I
stood. She grabbed the pitcher and dumped it on him, a gallon
of water and ice cubes crashing over his head and chest. He
groaned and opened his eyes. If he was acting he was doing a
good job of it. He got to his feet and shuffled off hanging his
head—she'd bested him again. Triumphant, she sent me to get
the mop and clean up.

A day came in July when Stanley put an end to all this
madness, a thirteen-year-old boy taking responsibility for a
frightened younger brother and two criminally irresponsible
adults. I was away from home for the day, working at Rowena's.
"I routinely bought the groceries," Stan explains. "She would
cut all these coupons out of the paper and mark everything on
sale in the ads and then I would go to the various stores on my
green bicycle with the big basket. Let me preface this by saying
that in her mind there was a long list of injustices that we'd

done her, okay? At this period in time she felt that we were trying to get back at her. So on this particular day, among other items, I'd had to purchase some buttermilk." The waxboard buttermilk carton, in the bottom of the brown paper grocery sack, had rubbed against the bicycle basket wires on the long trek from store to store. "When I got home the buttermilk had started leaking. She claimed that I'd opened it up and poisoned it. There was a lot more to it because she built this paranoid case up while she was eating watermelon. I was sitting there just as hungry as I could be and I asked for some, several times I think, and she said, 'Well, you're not getting any watermelon.' She accused me of poisoning the buttermilk and of trying to do some other things—I don't remember clearly what those were because it was a long harangue at the time. She had a big belt with brass do-goodies all in it, studs, and she began beating me with it and she just beat me and beat me. I just couldn't take it. I couldn't bear it. If you beat an animal like that and beat it and beat it, it's going to run, right? So that was the mechanics of the thing. I ran out the back door and she ran after me trying to keep on beating me and when she went back in I ran back to the door, got the old bicycle and took it.

"I spent the day in the tunnels," Stan goes on. "I worked it out that there was no place to run away to. Nobody wanted me. That the only thing I *could* do was just turn myself in at the police station and tell them the whole story. That's what I did." Stanley knew the police station because we'd gone there to get licenses for our bikes. "I remember the police officer was a kindly, fatherly type. He just sort of shook his head a lot and listened a lot. I know he called the dress shop. I don't know who he talked to, but I said, 'I do not want to go home. No way.' He asked me where I wanted to go. I said, 'Well, I have an aunt.' Aunt Espy. It did occur to me that I could go there and live with them. I'd work for them on the farm, be a good boy and, you know, make my way with them. They said, 'No, we'd love to have you, but we can't, we can't afford you.' "

"Did you show him your welts?" I ask.

"I believe I did, yeah."

"And there was something to show?"

"Oh, of course. And he looked over my general condition, and I'm sure he summed that up rather accurately. And so he made phone calls and other stuff, and I just sat there a long, long time and finally he drove me downtown."

The social worker's version of Stanley's runaway introduces another conflict over food but fails to mention physical abuse and even coyly questions his judgment:

Problem:

The boy came to the police station and stated that his step mother mistreats him and his brother. That today she tried to whip him because he could not eat two eggs that had been boiled for over two weeks. She ran him out of the house with a belt. He states that he does not want to go back home and live with her. The boy told probation officer that maybe the eggs had not been cooked quite two weeks but he knows they have been cooked several days. There were dark marks on the eggs. He said the step mother and father have arguments in the home and it is mostly over the care of these two boys. The mother does forbid them to go to the ice box and he is just generally unhappy with her because she is too strict with him. He states his younger brother Richard is of the same opinion [but] that the step mother will give him a look and he will change his opinion. He [Richard] is afraid of her.

(I'm puzzled by the pitch of the social worker's two reports. They deliberately underplay the extremity of our situation. Possibly the woman was trying to be objective. I met her again when I was eighteen and about to graduate from Drumm. I had to return to court to be released from its jurisdiction. She cried with happiness for me and made it clear she'd understood we needed help. "We had a real dilemma," she told me. "You had a home and two parents. You weren't technically indigent and normally we wouldn't have removed you from a home with two parents. But I could see you'd both been starved. That's what I remember most of all, how terribly underweight you were. *She* obviously wasn't starved.") Stanley spent the next two weeks at the Jackson County juvenile detention center, a jail for delinquents but the only place the county had available in those days to stow children waiting for hearings. "Stanley is 5 ft 4 in tall and weighs 97 lbs," the social worker begins her summary of my brother's final ordeal. "He is a freshman. He is a very pleasant boy. He has been ill since in the juvenile court building. He had a sore throat, nausea, and some vomiting. He was taken to General Hospital receiving ward and checked. The doctors said it was a slight cold. They gave him a lot of fluids and rest." And this from a previous paragraph: "The boy is extremely emotional. When talked to about any matter he starts crying and hangs his head."

"I was just about sick the whole time," Stan recalls. "I had a real horrible case of the flu, and I was beaten up by another guy there who was much, much older. I was given a Bible early on and I was reading that Bible and for some reason that infuriated this guy. Well, for me it was something to do. I was bored out of my skull. These guys were tough guys, so he was going to prove it by beating me up. Between being sick and being beat up, I had very little feeling left. I was just a body practically. And this one guard says, 'Hey, we're going to lose this kid if you don't put him in some other place.' There was solitary confinement, so they put me in solitary confinement. They left the door open so I'd be free to go in and out. It was like a hospital bed basically in there. I lay in there for about a week, trying to recover. They brought me down to give me tests. I remember taking a Rorschach, a cartoon test, verbal tests, math tests, English tests, a whole series of tests. They tried their best to take care of me."

In the meantime I was still at home. After her initial rage subsided at Stanley's defection and she understood that she was up against the law, our stepmother set out to court me. My diet suddenly improved to include meat and potatoes. My table manners no longer offended her and I joined the family board. There was talk of buying me a camping chest and sending me to Boy Scout camp. I remember an evening in particular when she offered me strawberries. I told her I didn't want them.

"Why not?" she questioned me sharply.

"Because Stanley doesn't get any," I dared to say.

"Stanley doesn't deserve any," she spat. "He's telling them lies about me."

Not daring more, I ate the strawberries, glad for them, ashamed to be eating them, convinced I was betraying my brother. I rationalized that the detention center would be feeding him well.

She coached me to counter Stanley's charges. I saw that her fury for self-justification gave me a degree of control and played at negotiating. Stanley's telling them X, she would say, but you know very well what happened was Y, don't you? No, I would counter, what happened was Z, Z somewhere mediate between her version and the truth. Her anger would flicker and then withdraw. I was tickling a dragon's tail. It was a dangerous and corrupting game. The social worker understood I was compromised: "Richard had been dissatisfied at home," she reported after she interviewed me, "mostly since step mother returned from Leeds Sanitarium; at times he will say he wants to be away from home. Then his step mother will talk to him or do some nice thing for him and he will change again." Against all evidence, as if wishing might ever make it so, part of me still longed for a strong father and a loving mother, a happy home.

Stanley fought for both of us. "I remember saying on several occasions," he told me in Idaho, " 'I want to be with my brother. I'd like to see him out of there.' " He knew I had to be removed, against my will if necessary.

The time came for our day in court. I arrived with Dad and my stepmother. Someone, probably the social worker, led me away to the judge's chambers to meet Stanley. The judge's name was Riederer. He had red hair and I remember counting that coincidence a good omen. I didn't know what would happen. I wanted to be with Stanley, but I had promises in my pocket that things would improve and I didn't want to leave Dad.

Stan says the decision was already made, that the judge met with us in chambers only to confirm that we wanted relief, but I remember a more elaborate drama. I remember being offered a choice between Drumm and McCune, the county's home for juvenile delinquents. I remember choosing Drumm simply by elimination, because I'd been there once and McCune was a blank. Most vividly of all, I remember standing in open court with Stanley ahead of me before the bench where I couldn't see his eyes and with our stepmother seated directly behind me boring her fury into the small of my back. I remember Judge Riederer asking me formally if I wanted him to remove me with my brother or if I wanted to go home with my stepmother and my dad. I remember my flesh crawling as I searched for the

courage to repudiate her, my commandant, my seductive torturer, by casting myself out into the unknown. Could even the
judge and the law protect us from her? I almost faltered. I didn't
know if I'd be taken away immediately or have to go back home.
If I had to go back home even long enough to pack it might be
fatal. Stanley's straight, determined presence sustained me. "I
want to be with my brother," I finally said.

I didn't have to go home. Harry Nelson was waiting in the
judge's chambers to deliver us to safety. "The rest of the ses-
sion," says Stan, "was taken up with Granny Annie and Dad in
the courtroom. I saw them enter, and I waited and waited and
waited, and I saw them leave. She was extremely angry when
she was leaving. She said something about betrayal. That I had
told a bunch of lies on her." He talked to Dad about it long
afterward. "He never really was bitter toward me, but he did
say one thing, reproachfully. 'You sure made her look bad,' he
said."

Whistling the whole way the odd, tuneless whistle with
which we learned he filled any awkward silence, Mr. Nelson
drove us to Drumm. We pulled up in front of the brick dormitory
and dining room at two o'clock. We'd missed dinner. The housemother delivered us to the cook, who sat us down at a kitchen
table and began hauling leftovers out of the big white refrigerator
along the east wall: chicken-fried steak and cream gravy, new
potatoes boiled with green beans and ham, butter, raw country
milk, corn bread, caramel pudding. We dug in. "I've never seen
boys eat so much," the cook told me later. "You ate for most
of an hour. You was about starved." Safe for the first time in
years, beyond the reach of violence in a land of plenty, we ate
our fill.

3

Stages on Life's Way

Dear God, where gat these wild things wit?

—WILLIAM LANGLAND
Piers Plowman

1

I REMEMBER CLEARLY the first hours of that first day. Stanley and I finally finished eating. The cook called the head housemother. Mrs. Scraggs, who wore a starched white uniform, took us upstairs and assigned us beds in the east dormitory, Stanley's at the end of a row near a window, mine in the middle of the room near the frosted-glass hallway double doors. Mrs. Scraggs got linens from a hallway closet and showed us how to make our beds with the corners tucked and where to hang our towels. From the West Building she led us along a brick walk to the East Building and into the laundry room, which had a wall of numbered wooden compartments into which each boy's clothes were sorted when they came up from the commercial-scale laundry in the basement below. The laundry room was stacked with boxes and piles of new and used clothes from which Mrs. Scraggs issued us a wardrobe: white knit Jockey shorts with intricate pouches, white T-shirts, short-sleeved cotton print sport shirts, crisp blue-black jeans, freckled Rockford work socks with red heels and toes. Like rookies on a football team we inherited numbers other boys had used before us, stamping them into each item of clothing in a designated location so that the boys doing laundry could sort them. Months later a pair of jeans

meant for a six-footer, boy number 4 before me, recently graduated, would appear in my laundry box.

Our mounds of folded clothes seemed a bounty as generous
as the bounty of food the cook had served us. When we finished
with them they reeked of indelible ink. We carried them back
to the West Building and put them away.

Mrs. Scraggs dispatched us to the school building then, to
Mr. Nelson's office. We knocked on the door. He called us in
and motioned us into chairs. He'd been reflecting on our morning
in court, he told us when he looked up from the document he
was reading. Carefully he unhooked his spectacles from his ears
and leaned back, his chair squeaking. "Your stepmother is a
bad woman," he said, instantly winning our loyalty, "the worst
I've ever seen, and I've seen some bad ones." The court was
right to take us away. Our father could visit us once a month,
on visiting Sunday. He told us about the allowances we'd re-
ceive. Had we brought any money with us? We hadn't, not a
dime. If we had we were expected to turn it in. The Institute
would maintain a savings account for us until we graduated or
left.

He got up and came around his desk and led us upstairs
to a storage closet, whistling his tuneless whistle. The closet
was filled with shoe boxes. He guessed our sizes correctly and
fitted us with good leather shoes, high-topped black work shoes
and brown dress shoes which he cautioned us to wear only for
school and town. From the attic he brought down glossy black
rubberized overshoes. We were expected to wear them to protect
our work shoes whenever we worked in the barns or in wet fields.
Never forget or lose them, he told us keenly.

Down to the school building basement we followed his
whistle. I thought of the Seven Dwarfs, or at least I think of

them now, two starved, battle-fatigued boys and this leonine, barrel-chested, bandy-legged little man. He built up the foot controls of his car with rubber shoe heels on the brake and clutch pedals and a rubber doorstop on the accelerator to bring them within range of his feet, but he had cultivated a commanding presence across twenty years of superintending; we learned to respect him. He brooked no nonsense from anyone, not even bullyboys half again his size.

In the basement shop Mr. Nelson unlocked a green cabinet and brought out a sheet of light aluminum and a set of numbered steel punch dies. He fetched tin shears from a mounting on the wall and showed us how to cut aluminum strips the size of return-address labels. With the punch dies and a hammer we stamped our laundry numbers into the soft strips. Working on one of the big wooden benches that crowded one side of the basement, we punched holes in the uppers of our overshoes, attached our aluminum labels with copper rivets and fanned the rivets with a ball peen hammer. The hammer and the shears hung among a panoply of tools mounted on brackets on a glossy green sheet of plywood mounted in turn on the wall. White paint silhouetted each tool so that even newly arrived innocents like the Rhodes brothers would know where to replace them. There were tools for carpentry, metalworking, plumbing and blacksmithing—a cascade of hammers, a phalanx of crescent wrenches, scales of screwdrivers, arpeggios of drill bits for wood and steel. I learned to use them all. Ten years later, testing for assignment in the Air Force Reserve among a competitive crowd of young New York lawyers, I opened my test booklet to a page of tool silhouettes and knew I'd hit the jackpot.

Mr. Nelson was a man of minute and creative frugality. Shoes were serious obligations. Stan remembers losing his work shoes on one of the annual camping trips we took. "We were camping at Big Spring State Park, down in the Ozarks. I tried to swim the Current River. I took off my shoes and tied them around my neck so that I wouldn't get them all wet. Swam in the water and they promptly got all wet, naturally. Not only that, but they went floating on down the river, lost forever. Oh God, was I in trouble. I knew I was sunk as soon as Nelson heard about it. There wasn't a thing I could do. I'd have to go to him for other shoes.

"But I had my old tennis shoes and the following week that vacation came up when you got a few days to visit your family or whatever. We went to Aunt Espy's. I told her my sad story and she promptly went out and bought me a pair of new work shoes as close to the original as she could find.

"About six months later I'd worn those shoes out. They had holes in them, crud all over them, and it was time to turn them in for a new pair. Nelson just looked at them and looked at them. He knew they were the wrong brand. He looked at them and he looked at me and he shook his head. He couldn't figure out how it had happened."

"Alien shoes from Mars," I interject.

"Right." Stan smiles. "So he took down a new pair and gave them to me and I went, *Whoo-boy*, that was the end of that. He never figured it out. Oh, I was lucky. Shoes were a fetish of his. I told Aunt Espy how grateful I was to her. It cost her ten or fifteen dollars."

Back at the West Building with shoes put away, dressed in my new work clothes, I decided I wanted to get going. Show Mr. Nelson I'd be useful around the place. Show him I wasn't a shirker. *Do you think you would care to live in the country,* the application form I'd filled out for Drumm had questioned,

and learn about farming? "Yes," I'd written. *Why?* the form
had persisted. "It's a good way to make a living," I'd answered
lamely, a stepmother answer. I marched over to the school
building and presented myself. Mr. Nelson looked up curiously.
I didn't have to do any work on my first day, he told me. But I
want to, I insisted. He twirled his spectacles between thumb
and forefinger, studying me, amused. "You could run an errand
for me," he said finally. "There's a crew down in the south
pasture cutting sod. Go and tell them it's time to come in for
chores."

I panicked. I didn't have the faintest idea what he was
talking about. I didn't know what a pasture was, what cutting
sod was or even which way was south. The blood roared in my
ears. He saw my confusion. "Here," he told me, rounding his
desk and throwing a muscular arm across my shoulders, "come
out onto the porch and I'll show you." He steered me out the
door. I was shaking. He pointed the way and explained. I saw
where he was pointing but couldn't hear his directions. Pretending to understand, I raced off.

I quartered the south pasture for most of an hour. I saw
not a sign of a crew. I couldn't have, since the crew was up
beyond the creek valley over the next hill, as Mr. Nelson had
explained. I was terrified. I was sure that if I failed at this first
assignment I'd be sent back to live with my stepmother. I swore
until I was sworn out. Then I began the serious bargaining. I
started to cry. I told God I was sorry I'd ever doubted Him. If
He allowed me to find the sod crew and deliver Mr. Nelson's
message, I promised I'd dedicate my life to Him. I believed in
Him now, I told Him. I chanted it. "I believe in You now. I
believe in You now."

But there was no crew to be found, and eventually, hearing

the dinner bell, I stumbled back to the school building. Mr. Nelson was just locking up. He was surprised to see me. He'd forgotten my errand. I blurted that I couldn't find the crew. He looked at me over his spectacles. "They came in an hour ago," he said, not unkindly. "You'd better go along and get cleaned up for supper." I went along, unpunished and relieved, uncertain where my bargain stood with God, and sat shyly to supper with thirty other boys—meat and potatoes, green beans, hot corn bread, stainless-steel pitchers of strong-tasting raw milk, second helpings if we wanted, loaves and fishes—on the evening of the first day.

The Andrew Drumm Institute was the invention of a pioneer Kansas City cattleman, established under a trust in Andrew Drumm's will when he died in 1919 at ninety-one.* His will doesn't explain why he chose to invest his substantial estate in such an unlikely project. One of his friends passed down the story that Andy Drumm had seen homeless children sleeping in doorways in downtown Kansas City. "I'll do something about that," he'd responded. Drumm and the young wife he married in middle age, Cordelia, were childless; discovering children abandoned when they had none of their own may explain his indignation. He visited private orphanages in Chicago, Philadelphia and Baltimore looking for a model. He seems to have found it in the McDonough Institute in Baltimore, home to some 115 boys when he visited it, that was also an eight-hundred-acre working farm. In his will Drumm apportioned Cordelia $150,000—a comfortable endowment for the rest of her life in 1919 dollars; it would be twenty times that today—and bequeathed the balance of his self-made wealth, about

*Information on Andrew Drumm from George C. Berkemeier, *Major Andrew Drumm 1828–1919*, privately printed, 1976.

$1,800,000, to establish an institution "for the maintenance, care, education and protection of Orphan and indigent boys."

"They shall not be made to feel that they are objects of dependence," Drumm specified, "but that they are doing something for themselves in the Institute." We wore no uniforms; he preferred us "plainly, decently, but not distinctively clad." The character of our education was to be "most thorough and practical," but he didn't wish us isolated, and stipulated that we should attend public schools. In exchange for being fed, clothed, housed and educated we were expected to work:

> The youth who may be received in the Institute shall be required and trained to care for themselves as much as is consistent with their age and good discipline. They shall be required to assist in the cultivation of as much of the land as may be thought best by the trustees and in the raising of fruit, vegetables, flowers, hay, cereals, poultry, cattle, swine and such other products and things that can be cultivated, manufactured or raised with profit or for the best education of the youth. . . .

The old pioneer, who had supplied beef and pork to the miners of the California gold rush and doubled his money running longhorns up from Texas to Kansas in the early days of the cattle drives, who had slept under the stars more often than under a roof until he was past fifty, had the pleasure of acquiring the land for his utopia before he died, making the word flesh. In 1912, for $85,000, he bought a showplace 360-acre farm just south of Independence, Missouri, in eastern Jackson County. Its improvements included a long white horse barn and a bank barn big enough to winter a herd of cattle, a limestone smokehouse squat and square as a jail, fields of grain and sweeping bluegrass pastures. A substantial twelve-room brick house, Missouri Colonial in style, crowned the hill at the center of the property. Constructed in the early 1880s of bricks kilned on the site, it had a massive slate roof, six attic bays, eleven fireplaces, indoor plumbing, speaking tubes connecting the rooms and a graceful, white-columned porch wide as the house, which looked east through a hillside park of trees toward the old road between Independence and the town of Lee's Summit. It became the East Building, the first residence hall at the new institute.

To these original improvements the trustees Drumm appointed in his will added a second residence hall, the West Building, a fireproof Colonial of brick and concrete and stone. The kitchen was in the West Building. It opened onto a dining room that seated fifty people. A living room off-limits except on Sundays after church and a recreation room where we passed rainy evenings listening to the radio occupied the other side of the first floor. On the second floor, a houseparent apartment divided the two bedroom wings into an east dormitory and a west, each of which held twelve beds, twelve bedside chests and twelve wardrobes. The dormitory and bathroom floors were terrazzo, the showers and toilets partitioned off with stone slabs. The building's monumental construction would have survived a tornado; from flying through space I'd touched down on bedrock.

The two residence halls faced one side of an oval drive. The new brick school building with its classroom and study hall, Mr. Nelson's office, an upstairs infirmary and a basement workshop had just been finished on the other side of the oval the summer we arrived. West beyond the drive was the original horse barn, the upper barn now, enlarged with a dairy wing and a machine shed not long after Drumm opened its doors in 1929. A wide gravel lane led south from the upper barn to the lower cattle barn. Round white silos with conical shingle roofs like the towers of Normandy châteaus had been backfitted onto both barns. That summer the boys had disassembled a war-surplus barracks on an air base in central Missouri, trucked it home and reassembled it as a slaughter- and canning house along the lane between the two barns next to a low, white, green-shingled chicken house that held some 250 white leghorn laying hens. A twenty-acre garden spread its bounty west beyond the slaughter- and chicken houses: a vineyard of Concord grapes for jelly-making, beds of asparagus blown in midsummer to fern, rows of dark green potato plants hazed with purple-white flowers, acres of beans and tomatoes staked high as leafy hedges. More acres of strawberries vegetated in a second garden farther west and there were peach, pear and apple trees in an orchard out of sight over the hill beyond the valley of the south pasture, near where the crew I couldn't find had been cutting sod. Roan shorthorn cows and calves ruminated under monumental elms in the south pasture creek valley. Hogs sprawled on a mud-crusted patch of pasture within shouting distance of their slop troughs behind the upper-barn machine shed. Dairy cattle and sheep grazed the pasture north of the school building, where the boys were building a pond.

I absorbed this beneficence operationally, in and through my body, and the learning took years. Food, work, terrain, weather and people surrounded me and passed through me. My hands comprehended the shape of what they grasped, my muscles measured the resistance of what they pushed and pulled and lifted. There was a child went forth every day, Walt Whitman declares, and all that he looked upon became part of him. I was that child. At Drumm I was that child. I opened into the world and incorporated it. I deflated and solidified and filled.

Drumm's 1949 camping trip was scheduled to begin just two weeks after Stanley and I arrived. Since the trip was supposed to reward a summer of farm work, Mr. Nelson debated whether to allow us along. He did; I think he decided we'd be useless left behind.

Drumm camping trips went everywhere, but this one, marking the one hundredth anniversary of the California gold rush, was exceptional even among its kind. In two weeks of travel and camping we would follow the Santa Fe Trail to New Mexico and on into Arizona, ranging as far west as the Grand Canyon and as far south as Carlsbad Caverns. Most of the trip is a blur to me now, mixed up with other camping trips in other years, but I remember stops along the way. We traveled in caravan: Mr. Nelson's black Chevy, a green five-ton truck with a home-made green doghouse on the back that carried our ton of staples and our tents, a new green school bus and a green passenger van we called the carryall. Twenty-eight boys that trip. The little boys rode in the carryall and I rode among them. Stanley was old enough for the bus; it was strange to be away from him, to see him through a crowd, to sleep away from him, to lose track of him from day to day.

The first or second night out we stopped in southern Kansas at Drumm Pastures, a vast ranch the Institute owned, punched with oil wells, that it leased for cattle grazing. A prairie line storm caught us before we had time to set up our tents. We found cover in an abandoned ranch house, not much more than a shed, two bare rooms littered with mouse nests under a leaky roof. We ate a cold supper instead of the traditional nightly corned-beef stew—corned-beef sandwiches, probably, God help our bowels, and canned fruit salad. George Berkemeier was Drumm's vocational agriculture teacher and unofficial assistant

superintendent then, forty years old, nearly bald, the solid, unflappable son of a German farmer, with a big grin, a long jaw and penetrating blue eyes; he and Mr. Nelson and a young college-student housefather, the adults on this adventure, worked to crowd all twenty-eight of us in under the ranch-house roof. Fitting our sleeping bags around the leaks gave the men a human jigsaw puzzle to solve. When we were all positioned they went off through the downpour to sleep in the vehicles. Lightning flashed off the rolling buffalo prairie and thunder exploded. It was a blowing, phantasmagoric night. It saturated my senses, a view beyond the valley of the shadow where Stanley and I had languished just weeks ago. Bewildered though I was, still dazed, I yet understood somewhere beneath consciousness that I had drawn a lucky hand at last, that I had been transported beyond danger into some benevolent stranger's sturdy countrified utopia.

But I was far from healed. From some of that past there will never be any final healing. We rolled out the next morning and headed on down toward Santa Fe. A few days later we camped at nine thousand feet in the Sangre de Cristos, the last campsite left in the park. We rushed to start our stew—fifteen pounds of canned corned beef, half a bushel of potatoes, two dozen onions, two dozen carrots, two heads of cabbage and a dozen turnips—boiled it for two hours and ate burned potatoes raw. In Santa Fe, timidly but with great determination, I bought a little souvenir bow and arrow from a sidewalk Indian. It must have cost my entire allowance. We camped overnight in the Painted Desert and posed for our group picture in the Petrified Forest standing and sitting along a million-year-old log.

Another storm blew up at the Grand Canyon. I was feeling vertiginous anyway, walking the trail along the South Rim, and the wind gusting at my back seemed to push me toward the drop-off. I had caught a lizard a few moments before the wind came up; it had shocked me by snapping off its tail and sprinting away with the bloody stump and I had felt guilty for injuring it, not knowing lizards shed their tails routinely in defense. Wild and beautiful the deep canyon was, I was sensible to that, but it was also the treacherous canyon of my childhood nightmare, which may be what drew me, the pleasant roadside stream that dropped to a torrent running far below, the cliff over which I fell. I tried to back away. Slogging through nightmare, my legs hardly worked. I forced myself away and stayed away.

We caravaned south to Carlsbad. There was a large crowd of tourists ahead of us at the caverns that August morning and we had to wait an hour for a tour. We were lucky we did; the resident bats returned late from their night of foraging while we waited and we got to watch them gyring into the cave mouth, the largest bat population in North America. They were so black against the bright desert morning, they flickered by so peripherally, that they seemed less animals than compulsive knife wounds stabbed through the fabric of the air.

We descended into the caverns down a long, winding ramp. The entrance disappeared around a bend. Spotlights lit the huge stalagmite columns from below, casting gigantic shadows. We moved deeper into the darkening labyrinth until the ranger who was guiding us stopped us. The caverns had been dark for fifteen million years, he told us through his megaphone. He would turn off the lights now for thirty seconds to show us that aboriginal darkness; he asked us to respect the silence of the caverns with silence.

I wasn't ready when the lights went out. I was standing alone, a little separate from the others, and abruptly the world itself was torn away around me; I couldn't see my hand an inch from my eyes. It was worse than Stanley's tunnels. I was alone, lost underground in the largest caverns in North America, depths still unexplored, a hole in the earth unbounded. I was ready to cry out when my eyes adjusted enough to find a faint glow coming through a crack in the ceiling far above me. That hope of rescue contained me until the ranger's interminable thirty seconds passed and he turned the lights back on. We toured the innards of the great beast then, down through the levels, fantastic formations like the wallpaper creatures of my childhood embossed from the wall into fully rounded rock. I loved rock. Rock was solid. However precariously I might balance on the rim of nightmare, the view into the depths enthralled me: terror was there certainly, but almost unbearable beauty was there as well. And more to come, farming to come, plants and animals in their tarantellas of birth and flourishing and harvest-death; and I see now I was Miranda and Caliban both, the child who went forth and the farting dumb cluck, lucky me, the one corrected and balanced the other.

CHAPTER

2

EVERY BOY AT DRUMM had chores, work to do twice a day, after breakfast and before supper. By tradition the noblest chore, reserved for responsible juniors and seniors, was milking cows. Farther down the line came feeding and herding cattle, hogs, sheep and horses and cleaning out the barns. From mammals to chickens was a descent; gathering eggs and cleaning chicken roosts was low work.

Small boys and new boys picked up odds and ends for chores, learning the ropes. Our first two months at Drumm, Stanley and I joined a crew straightening nails for reuse salvaged by the kegful from a demolished work shed. We prided ourselves on the blood-blistered fingers we acquired. In the new school building workshop Mr. Berkemeier directed a team of older boys making bedside wooden storage chests for the West Building dormitories, and it began to look as if we apprentices would spend a long, boring winter hand-sanding homegrown black walnut boards for chores. Fortunately Mr. Berkemeier was also preparing to frame mountings of the hundreds of prize ribbons, purple and blue and red and white and yellow, that the Drumm boys had won over the years in Future Farmers of America and 4-H competitions, to decorate the walls of the new school building classroom. He needed a team to organize the ribbons, type labels for them on an old office Underwood and glue them into place. Stanley and I eagerly volunteered, and since we were comparatively scholarly and not yet qualified for serious work, we got the job. If it lasted through the winter we could spend the cold months choring in the warm classroom; we stretched it all the way to February.

Stanley went on then to regular chores—chickens, probably, the starter chore I'd be assigned a few months down the road and be stuck with for two years. I joined the apprentices Mr. Berkemeier kept at his side. He was training us, but I realize now he was also baby-sitting. Before the first sign of spring obvious enough for me to recognize (serious spring begins in Missouri in March), he set us to building a hotbed on the south side of the chicken house at the edge of the garden. We staked up a frame of one-by-six boards the size of a double bed and dug a pit three feet deep within the perimeter of framing. We drove pitchforks down into a crusty mountain of straw-matted horse manure piled outside the upper barn, extracted manure hot from fermentation and hauled the steaming clumps by the wheelbarrow load to the pit we'd dug. There we built up a thick layer, bulking it with fresh straw and pouring in hot water to boost the fermentation. We topped off the hotbed with four inches of fine black loam from the garden, mixing it with sand. Mr. Berkemeier had big hands with thick, bent thumbs; I was impressed with the attention he gave to the soil in the seedbed we were preparing, combing his fingers again and again through the top layer, sifting out rocks and breaking up clods. We didn't bother to take the soil temperature, but with its boost of fermentation it would have measured warm enough to germinate seeds, which was the point. We planted the hotbed with seeds of tomato and cabbage, to grow sets to plant in the garden later in the spring, and covered it with a frame of glass panes overlapped to keep out snow and cold but let in the sun. It was old technology, nothing like the warp-drive rockets of the pulp science fiction I had consumed in the city, but I could handle it and see it and smell it, it generated heat mysteriously and spontaneously from waste, and when the first sprouts appeared, delicate as small butterflies, I was converted.

One morning Mr. Berkemeier handed me an old butcher knife and a bushel basket and led me down past the chicken house and the hotbed to the lower quarter of the garden. He pointed out a row mounded wide with a dry crust of horse manure that ran west to the far end. Thick, pale stalks of asparagus poking through the crust zigzagged at random intervals down the row. Mr. Berkemeier showed me how to cut them, stabbing the butcher knife into the crust to sever their buried shanks. He made sure I knew what I was doing and left me to the work. I'd never seen asparagus before and didn't immediately learn to like its strong taste and the strong odor it lent to my urine, but I loved the chore of harvesting it. It was the first vegetable of spring, bursting from the ground with such insistence that it broke back the hard crust of manure that dressed it. It grew luxuriantly; I had to cut it immediately after breakfast, before the sun had risen over the trees east of the garden, or it would green and elongate and toughen almost before my eyes. Any stalk I missed would already have begun to spray itself to fern by the following morning. The one drawback to asparagus harvesting was that the shorter and thicker stalks among its variety looked enough like the erections of a preadolescent boy to be embarrassing to find and to handle. I hauled a bushel basket or more of asparagus to the kitchen every day.

Cutting asparagus was a limited, half-time chore. I don't remember what else I did that first spring. One of my early chores was herding a flock of sheep onto the yard grass around the residence buildings mornings and evenings to graze. I thought sheep were the dumbest animals on the farm until I got involved with chickens. If one sheep crossed the road from one area of yard to another, the entire herd followed, bleating and dropping their trails of glossy black pills. They were difficult to keep together, difficult to move from place to place, difficult to return to their barn lot mornings in time to get ready for school. The Drumm dogs might have helped, but like the Drumm boys they were mutts and strays short on farm experience. I laughed in revenge when I saw the sheep sheared that summer; stripped of their dignified wool, thin-shanked, knobby-kneed and bulbous, they looked as ridiculous as they behaved. (The custom shearer, a weather-beaten old alcoholic who could flip a ewe onto its back and clip off its wool in one piece in under ten minutes, had the most beautiful hands I'd ever seen. They'd soaked for decades in raw lanolin; they looked like the praying hands that Albrecht Dürer drew.)

The most intimidating chore Mr. Berkemeier assigned me in my first year at Drumm was moving the roan shorthorn herd bull from its feedlot in the lower barn up the lane to the north pasture, where it spent the day among Drumm's sixty registered cows, happily breeding. The herd bull weighed something close to a ton. Its horned head was massive. It had no neck at all. Its shoulders and flanks rippled with muscle; its hooves crushed gravel where it walked. On the way to open the lower barn gate, the boy whom Mr. Berkemeier detailed to train me pulled a pitiful length of stick, hardly more than a switch, from a fence where he'd stuck it. "Ain't no problem," he told me when he saw the look on my face. "He knows where he's going. Alls you got to do is walk along where he can see you and make sure he don't wander off." The bull was waiting at the gate when we arrived, eager to begin the day. That was an obstacle because the gate opened inward. The boy poked his stick through the slats to back the bull off, opened the gate enough to let it out and whacked it nonchalantly into position along the lane fence, where its daily perambulations had worn a path in the crabgrass that grew in the fence margins. It proceeded ponderously up the path, head down, shoulders and flanks rolling, its mighty scrotum swinging left and right in rhythm. "He's what you might call *motivated*," the boy winked at me. But my God the animal was large.

It had some sort of Classical Greek name—Apollo? Hector? Zeus? I accompanied old Agamemnon from the lower barn to the north pasture and from the north pasture back down to the lower barn twice a day until the end of breeding season. Giant though it was, it was peaceful and even serene, particularly in the evening ambling home from work. I came to feel comfortable in its presence. Walking it wasn't exactly the same as walking a dog or even a horse. A dog would have been obsequious, a horse independent, both more or less under control. Walking a herd bull was more like walking an ocean liner, knowing that you guided it only because it was headed in your direction anyway. I had trouble with the animal just once, when I stupidly forgot to check a gate in a corner where the fence turned ninety degrees right. The bull turned to follow the fence, found no fence where the gate was open, rotated on through the opening and headed up the path on the other side, a path we used to go to chores that led past an incinerator and a beehive through a grove of trees to the West Building. There was no turning my ponderous charge around. I took off running for help. A couple of seniors on their way to the dairy barn came to my rescue. Once the bull emerged from the grove of trees it could see the cows in the north pasture, and once it saw the cows it headed straight north for the pasture fence. Then it only had to be driven along the fence to the barn and turned through the barn into the pasture. I was grateful it had the courage of its convictions. I never again forgot to check the gate.

We planted leaf lettuce and carrots and radishes and scallions. We planted peas and string beans and head lettuce and corn. We planted onions, cucumbers, lima beans, potatoes, beets, squash, cantaloupe, pumpkin. We planted the tomato sets from our hotbed, long rows plowed and then disked and harrowed smooth, mounded by hand with hoes, holes scooped out, boys following down the row with five-gallon buckets of water dipping water for the holes with number-ten cans, other boys bringing along wooden trays filled with small vigorous tomato sets, Mr. Berkemeier picking a set from a tray, gently lowering its mouse nest of roots into a muddy hole, pushing the loose dirt together around the stem to hold the plant upright, tamping down the dirt, moving on. We planted a twenty-acre garden that way each spring. The black soil greened and disappeared under a dark, fragrant feather bed of leaves that soughed in the breeze; looking out across it when I passed in the lane filled me with contentment.

Every boy at Drumm had an annual project. Two annual projects, actually, one for 4-H, one for FFA, the rural equivalent of Junior Achievement except that we functioned as individual entrepreneurs, as farmers do. Older boys raised animals, sheep one year, hogs the next, culminating in a 4-H/FFA fat calf when they were seniors. Younger boys raised vegetables. Along with my classmates I bought and planted a sack of seed potatoes that first year. They looked anything but promising; they were small and shriveled and dyed an ugly purple with potassium permanganate to kill any disease organisms they might have been carrying. I had no idea what would become of them. I hadn't seen a harvest yet; I was investing in potatoes by faith, doing what I was told. For a short-term payoff I had part of a black loam garden row to call my own, my first property, a piece of rented land.

Garden work occupied us throughout the summer. My potatoes sprouted and unfurled bushes with dark velvet leaves. I weeded them in the evening after other work, watered them when the rains came up short, picked off the Chinese red, black-spotted potato beetles and furry black caterpillars that thirsted for their juice. I understood intellectually that they were working underground, making potatoes, but I only experienced their fluffy superstructures. By comparison with the battalions of tomato vines bandoliered with red fruit that dominated the north end of the garden they appeared to be merely ornamental. I still cherished them, as pets are cherished, because they depended on me, because they were mine.

Tomatoes were the great harvest those summers, the human equivalent to elevators bursting with grain. I'd never seen so many tomatoes in my life. Outside in the hot summer sun I'd walk down a long row of tomato plants dragging a bushel basket behind me by one of its wire handles (or by the slatted brim if the handle was gone), other boys paralleling me in other rows. We hadn't staked the plants. They covered the ground and spread out their skirts into the rows. I picked each plant in turn clean of that day's ripe tomatoes. That was easy enough for the tomatoes on top, harder for the tomatoes underneath since I bent from the waist to avoid kneeling in the damp black dirt, saving my jeans. The vines were heavy to lift and I was squeamish about reaching back too far under them, afraid I might plunge my fingers into a rotten tomato set to burst at a touch like a land mine and spill a gush of foul liquid across my hand.

There were so many tomatoes to pick down those long garden rows that we made a contest of finding tomato rarities, freaks. I discovered two tomatoes grown together like a dumb-bell, a red giant swollen to cantaloupe scale that I had to use both hands to pick up, fully ripe midgets no larger than cherries, a tomato with a navel like an orange. We lined up our sports along a shelf in the canning house, a vegetable sideshow, freaks by the dozen, no lack of hermaphroditic mimics among them to license us yokels to nudge each other and laugh.

For canning, a crew of us under Mr. Berkemeier's super-vision moved a waist-high wooden trough with worktable wings out into the middle of the canning house and fitted ourselves with canvas aprons and paring knives. We set our bushel baskets on the floor near the black iron eight-burner cookstove in the south corner and took up workstations along the trough. The boy in charge of scalding the tomatoes loaded them into a wire basket that he dipped into one of the kettles of water boiling on the stove. When the scalded skin began to split he hauled the wire basket to the canning table and dumped it onto the wings. Red as blood, their glossy skins peeling, the steaming fruits came rolling my way. I picked up one and juggled it—the skin was hot enough to burn my fingers—stripped it to its cooler velvet meat, cored it, dropped it into the trough and picked up another. The acid pink juice ran down my hands and arms and dripped off my elbows. It made them itch; flapping them against my white T-shirt to relieve them stained my shirt red.

Once we got under way, mounds of lush tomatoes slumped down the sloping trough to one end and formed a terminal moraine where boys forced scoops of meat through belled funnels into hot mason jars, capped the jars with a rubber ring and a glass top, snapped a metal clamp over the glass and moved the jars to a cast-iron pressure cooker large as an oil barrel to sterilize them. At noon and again at the end of the day, though we had processed a continent of tomatoes by now, we sat on baskets turned upside down to make stools and sorted among the tomatoes still warm from the garden, found the best—the ripest and most perfectly formed—sprinkled them with coarse cattle salt and ate our fill, fine young cannibals, raw juice running from our mouths.

We picked acres of strawberries on our hands and knees, a dozen boys at a time crawling slowly across a strawberry patch toward the horizon, and sliced the bounty of those acres into sugar syrup for freezing. We froze rhubarb and lima beans and corn. We canned green beans and beets. We shelled peas until our thumbs were sore and put them up by the hundreds of freezer bags. We poured buckets of brine over cabbage chopped into a wooden barrel to make sauerkraut. We processed peaches in the same white enameled trough where we had processed tomatoes earlier in the summer and in nearly equal quantities, bagging them in syrup for freezing. I once spent an entire day slicing cucumbers for bread-and-butter pickles; by the end of the day the outer layer of skin on my hands had slipped painlessly away, exposing a pink and tingling fresh layer. From the orchard we harvested a wagonload of tart Jonathan apples that we stored spread out on a slatted wooden bed underground in the root cellar sodded over like a barrow, west of the school building. We hauled bushels of fine firm onions into the root cellar and tumbled them onto another bed, rolling and colliding, their yellow skins crackling complaint.

Finally it was time to harvest our potatoes. By then the plants had collapsed and spread out desiccated on the mound of the row like divinatory entrails. The farm manager, Mr. Taggart, a weathered Marlboro man in his early forties, harnessed a big dappled-gray Percheron that was one of the two remaining workhorses on the farm, led it out into the garden, hooked its traces to the singletree of the garden plow and lined up horse and plow at the head of our project row. We'd carried a pile of folded gunnysacks from the canning house. They'd been used before; dirt like gunpowder sifted through their coarse burlap when we shook them out, blackening our arms.

Mr. Taggart called "Gid'yup" and nicked to start the ceremony. The horse stepped forward, Mr. Taggart set the plowshare, the horse felt the resistance and leaned into it, the plowshare plunged into the mounded earth of the row with Mr. Taggart bending his weight over the handles to hold it down, the shiny, curving moldboard began to turn a furrow—and from the turning black mold in bounty emerged ivory potatoes fat as fists, potatoes like loaves, like dragon's teeth, like the stones of a hidden streambed revealed. My patch started farther down the row, so I could watch and learn. One boy and then another stumbled in the loose dirt of the furrow, following the plow, picking their potatoes eagerly and stuffing them into gunnysacks.

My turn came. By then I was ready. The plow opened back a black lip of earth to uncover potatoes secure in their buntings of loam as snuggled babies, dried umbilicals linking them to the exhausted plants above. I had sown so few and such shriveled seeds and here was a paradoxical munificence of foundlings. I stepped into the furrow, hooked my left arm inside the mouth of my gunnysack as I had learned to do to hold it open and began gathering my harvest. My potatoes were young and firm, warm, fresh with the healthy smell of earth. I cleaned them of clods with my thumbs. When I'd thoroughly picked the loose mold of potatoes I knelt in the furrow and dug more from the side of the cut. We needed hoes to finish the work. Down that short distance of garden row I loaded four gunnysacks of potatoes, four hundred pounds; our sacks stood guard along the rows like megaliths. We helped each other load them onto a cart and wheel them over to the north wall of the canning house, where we leaned them against the wall and Mr. Taggart showed us how to tie them off with lengths of twine.

Mr. Berkemeier pronounced that year's potato project a success, a bumper crop. We each picked out a class of our best potatoes to exhibit at the 4-H club fair and sold the rest to Drumm. I lingered over mine, sorting and arranging them. I hated to let them go. But into the root cellar they went with the apples and the onions. The root cellar became an earthy cornucopia provisioned against the long months of cold. When I worked on kitchen that winter I volunteered to fetch the day's requirements of root vegetables from the cellar even if doing so meant wading through the snow. Alone down in the cellar I would load a bucket of the best potatoes, not neglecting the smaller ones, and eat a crisp, sweet apple. Dug into the ground below the frost line, the root cellar was an easy place to linger. It was warmer there among the harvest of fruit and tubers than out in the open on the hard, frozen earth.

IT WOULD MAKE ME HAPPY to tell you that moving to Drumm healed Stanley and me of the wounds our stepmother inflicted on us. Drumm at least started the process of healing. It fed us and clothed us; we filled out to our normal weights. From a cold, empty world, from a concentration camp, it removed us to an institution set down in the midst of a bountiful farm, a world replete with food. It taught us skills that empowered us, lifting us from helplessness. I catalogued some of those skills in the introduction to my first book, *The Inland Ground*, published in 1970 when I was thirty-three:

> Began cleaning chicken roosts for chores, leading the old mare in and out of the barn to raise and lower the hay hook, straightening whole kegs of nails salvaged from a razed shed, hoeing the forty-acre garden [*sic*: hungry children have big eyes], picking strawberries, planting potatoes, filling up, when the train bell atop the smokehouse called us to supper, on heavy country food. Learning, later, to plow and disk and mow; to feed cattle and clean the barn; to cook for forty people and clean the dormitories; to cut down trees; to weld; to speak in public and conduct a parliamentary meeting; to operate a mangle and a steam press; to drive a school bus and a farm truck; to show a steer and a sheep; to butcher cattle and hogs and chickens;

That is six years of learning, a sample of six years, and it was good to learn, useful especially to a writer.

But all was far from well with me. I haven't said, though it ought to be obvious by now, that at Drumm we raised almost all of our food. Mr. Nelson allowed the head housemother, who managed the kitchen, to order staples such as flour, rice, cornmeal, dried beans, citrus juices, breakfast cereals and, rarely, white bread. Everything else in our larder was homegrown. Which means that we not only gardened, we also raised and slaughtered animals and cut up their meat. And in the course of time I had much to do with that.

In a privately printed volume that celebrates the first fifty years of the Andrew Drumm Institute I found a summary of inventories that illustrates the volume of farm products we processed. It doesn't precisely fit my years at Drumm—it covers 1948 through 1952, and I was there from 1949 to 1955—but it substantially overlaps. From 1948 through 1952, Drumm boys under the supervision of Mr. Nelson and Mr. Berkemeier processed 316,000 pounds of milk, 16,700 dozen eggs, 1,943 chickens, 22,882 pounds of beef (roughly 60 steers), 35,171 pounds of pork (roughly 200 hogs). Add the meat totals together and you will find that someone had to kill, bleed, flay, gut and dismember about 2,200 animals. I wasn't responsible for nearly that many acts of sanctioned violence in my years at Drumm, but I certainly did more than my share. I was shy and quiet, pious to the point of priggishness, beginning to imagine that I might be destined for the Methodist ministry, an outstanding student, a polite and dutiful boy. At the same time I demonstrated a talent, even a zeal, for the processing of animals into meat. Mr. Berkemeier noticed; in my last two years at Drumm, he frequently assigned me to lead the slaughter team.

Slaughtering wasn't easy to learn. It was never really easy to do. The skills involved were straightforward, an apprenticeship in dissection. But because of my past experience, I found the emotional iconography disturbing. It might be for anyone, I don't know. I've watched farmers castrating calves; they identify like crazy, playfully threatening each other with similar mutilations and hauling out every lame castration joke they've ever heard. Slaughtering is even worse. Slaughtering, however socially useful, is primordial death and dismemberment. I can't believe anyone does it without mobilizing a fair measure of dread.

We learned the rudiments of the trade on chickens. I spent my first two years at Drumm choring the chickens, white leghorns with scaly yellow feet, pale yellow beaks and beady red eyes. Our laying hens were confined in a square, one-story chicken house with wooden roosts raised up on a platform, a concrete floor bedded deeply with straw and southern-facing windows glazed to admit ultraviolet as well as visible light. We kept no roosters, raising our hens from day-old chicks bought at a hatchery and brooded under lamps; they laid sterile eggs. I hauled ground corn in five-gallon buckets twice a day to fill their self-feeders and washed and refilled their watering pans with water drawn from a freestanding faucet installed just outside the chicken-house door. Periodically I strewed their bedding straw with fresh alfalfa hay to supplement their diet and topped up their gravel bins with coarsely ground oyster shell; since they lacked teeth, they swallowed the gravel into a pouch at the base of their necks, called a craw, where it ground their feed and released calcium which their bodies recycled into the shells of their eggs. I scraped several five-gallon buckets of droppings from the waist-high platform below their roosts every morning and dumped them into an old iron-wheeled manure spreader we kept parked conveniently outside the chicken-house door. From nests built under the roosting platform I collected their daily production of eggs, something like 150 to 200 eggs for a flock of about 250 hens. Egg laying was a barometer of the flock's collective state of mind; it was sensitive to the season and the weather and to emotional stress as well. I learned to open the door into the chicken house slowly and to move deliberately while I worked. If a barking dog or a sonic boom startled the hens and sent them bawking and flapping madly against the walls, egg production dropped.

Chickens were the only animals on the farm I disliked. At first they frightened me. I was squeamish about the sticky, bitterly ammoniac manure that they dropped on the roost platform and the bedding straw in whitecapped burnt-umber daubs like oil paint squeezed from a tube. It was impossible to scrape the chicken roosts adequately without sometimes smearing a glove or the sleeve of my coat. I got over my squeamishness but I still didn't like the stink, which rose up from the straw as acrid dust whenever I moved through the chicken house and persisted in my nose and my hair all day.

Sometimes the hens pecked my hand when I reached under them to collect their eggs. Their beaks were sharp and the pecking hurt, a nasty pinch like the pinches my stepmother used to inflict. Collecting eggs made me shiver; when a hen pecked me I jumped back and danced. I wasn't fearful. I was shivering with rage. I retaliated by choking my attacker, immobilizing it while I removed its egg from the warm hollow of nest it defended. Choking worked so well I began applying it preemptively. Egg production began to decline. Mr. Berkemeier noticed and questioned me to see if he could identify a reason. I feigned ignorance, but I stopped choking the chickens. Production went back up.

Under conditions of confinement chickens can be cannibalistic. I came into the chicken house one day to find a chicken with its rear end partly pecked out, a bloody mess. The other chickens harassed it; it darted among them fearfully, trying to dodge their attacks. I was horrified. I looked up Mr. Berkemeier and reported what I'd found. "Well," he explained thoughtfully, "that happens sometimes. Catch it and put it into one of the cages and see if you can nurse it back to health." Watch for more victims, he directed me; contagion would signal a deficiency in the flock's diet that we'd need to correct.

I caught the injured chicken and made a nest for it in a chicken-wire cage built under the roosting platform at the end of the row of brood nests. I found a small pan for its water and another for its corn. But its vent was destroyed, I could see its intestines glistening through its exposed peritoneum and blood dripped from its massive wound. It wasn't even safe from attack. I came back later to find chickens pecking at it from below, through the wire floor of the cage, drawn by the blood. I identified with the wounded hen; the cruelty of its attackers made me furious. With equal cruelty I kicked them away. One big, persistent bully I strangled unconscious. By the next day the cannibalized hen was dead. One or two more showed up across my months of poultry husbandry, equally gruesome.

I came to hate chickens. I have no doubt now that I hated them because they reminded me of my stepmother. They were birds, not mammals, evolved with a different set of cues; I found their motives obscure. I didn't understand that stealing their eggs was challenging, that I provoked their attacks. They seemed to me implacably indifferent, cruel, malicious. The dissonance of their function disturbed me deeply: they were also maternal, warm in their nests, parturient with nurturing eggs. They were small enough to assault, but returning what I took to be their cruelty with cruelty freighted me with guilt. Their house was a prison for them and a halfway house for me. I felt reprieved when Mr. Berkemeier finally assigned me other chores.

Several times a year we culled the flock. Mr. Berkemeier taught us culling—identifying and separating from the flock those hens that had ceased laying eggs. We set up a partition in the chicken house on a Friday afternoon and moved all the hens to one side. One by one we caught and examined them. The comb and wattles of a leghorn hen that is laying are plump and bright red, its vent moist, the points of bone on each side of its vent spread three fingers or more wide to allow for the passage of its eggs. Its beak and feet are yellow-white because it concentrates most of the carotene that its diet of yellow corn and alfalfa supplies into the yolks of its eggs. When a hen stops laying, the carotene it ingests migrates to its beak and the scales of its feet and colors them darker yellow. Its pelvic space narrows to two fingers' width or less. Its vent and its comb and wattles wrinkle and dull. In most of the hens the difference was obvious. Mr. Berkemeier made the difficult calls. A crowd of culls, one hundred chickens or more, accumulated through the afternoon on the other side of the partition.

Saturday morning we slaughtered them. Slaughtering chickens required a substantial crew, ten or twelve boys in all. We divided up the work. One or two boys outside did the killing. One or two inside the slaughterhouse at great kettles of boiling water scalded the birds to loosen their feathers. Pickers at the first of a row of heavy butcher-block tables picked them clean, heaps of wet feathers billowing to the floor, and passed them along to boys who gutted them, cut them up and packaged them for freezing—Stanley sometimes, boys his age and older. When we slaughtered in the winter the air outside would be cold and dry, the air inside warm and steamy, dense with the smell of wet feathers and blood.

I turned formal and efficient when I butchered, walling off my feelings. We didn't use an ax or a hatchet to kill chickens; blood spurts from the neck of a decapitated chicken as it flaps and bucks in reflex, and unless the carcass is restrained it drenches itself in gore. In the scalding pot, the blood foams to a gray, greasy scum that fouls the feathers and makes plucking them repellent. For a cleaner kill we used a length of iron water pipe. I pinned back a chicken's wings with one hand, restrained its legs with the other, set my foot on one end of the pipe to tip the other end up, worked the chicken's neck under the pipe, clamped down the pipe with both feet and pulled. That left the head on the ground, the body bucking in my hands, and I could aim the torn neck away until the blood stopped spurting.

One of my classmates was crueler. He liked to set a carcass quickly on its feet after he decapitated it to watch it run around in circles in headless convulsion, flapping its wings and fountaining blood. That was funny, at about the same macabre level as castration jokes, the first once or twice he did it. After that we discouraged him; we didn't like the mess. Boys who barely contained their violence in the best of times came a little unglued on the slaughtering crews. They got skittish, giggly, wild. You watched out for their knives. I saw a boy once whack the back of another boy's hand with a butcher knife, laying open a serious wound. They'd been playing at stabbing the table between the spread fingers of each other's hands. The wounded boy ran bleeding for help. A few minutes later Mr. Nelson burst roaring into the slaughterhouse. He advanced bare-handed on the boy with the knife. The boy made the mistake of menacing it to threaten him, the only time I ever saw that happen at Drumm. Mr. Nelson didn't threaten. The boy was at least a foot taller than he, strong and dangerously armed, but Mr. Nelson jumped into his face, cleared the ground, wrapped his legs around the boy's chest, hauled on his hair, bowled him over, slammed the knife out of his hand, beat the back of his head against the concrete floor in rhythm to a string of euphemistic curses— "You half-wit! You quarter-wit! You stinking little punk! You think you can attack me with a knife?"—and when he'd subdued the boy he got to his feet, dusted himself off, pulled the miscreant up, shoved him toward the door and told him to get packed because he'd be off the premises permanently within the hour. And the poor dumb bastard was gone; we never saw him again.

Butchering hogs, eight or ten every three months, was coarse work. The two-hundred-pound carcasses had to be lowered with chains into a tank of scalding water wide as a rich man's grave, rolled one way and the other to loosen the hair and then hauled out and the hair scraped off. I choked on the stink of hogs; even castrated they smelled randy. In compensation, after the slaughtering was done and the carcasses had

211

been chilled out and cut up, we rendered lard. A stainless-steel lard-rendering vat, a beautiful double-walled cauldron shaped like an oversize kettledrum, was mounted permanently at one side of the slaughterhouse. A small boiler in an open bay next door that we fired with wood fed steam to the rendering vat's jacket. We filled it to the brim with the scraps of fat and skin we'd trimmed from the hog carcasses and built up the steam; half a day later we filtered buckets of hot, clear liquid out the rendering vat's spigot that cooled to the creamy white lard we used for cooking and baking. Left behind was a gallon or more of crunchy cracklings, pieces of deep-fried flesh like crumbled bacon without the smoky taste. We were growing boys; a handful of hot cracklings made our bellies smile.

Once a month we butchered a steer. I don't remember if Stanley and I worked together on a slaughtering crew; probably we did. Compared to butchering chickens and hogs, butchering a steer felt ceremonial. A fat steer ready for slaughtering weighed eight hundred pounds or more. For twenty-four hours ahead of time we isolated it in a separate pen in the lower barn to fast. On the morning of its sacrifice we closed all the gates and drove it slowly up the lane to the open ground outside the slaughter-house. It stopped in front of the building on a grassy patch and began to pull the grass with its black tongue. Mr. Taggart was waiting for us with a .22 rifle. We formed a wide circle like defensive linebackers, two younger boys and two older boys, the usual butchering team, getting out of the line of fire and positioning ourselves to head off the steer if the bullet didn't take it down. Mr. Taggart walked to within ten feet of the steer and raised the rifle to aim at the cross-point of an imaginary X he drew mentally between its eyes and its horns. Curious, the animal looked up to watch. We all got quiet. People always get quiet when they kill something as big as a steer. Mr. Taggart squeezed off a round.

I jumped at the report. The steer dropped like a puppet with its strings cut, its legs folding under it, and then it rolled over on one side and began to kick reflexively like a galloping horse. One of us took the rifle and passed Mr. Taggart a skinning knife sharp as a razor. He ran to the steer, hauled back its head and cut the animal's throat. Blood gushed out, the heart still pumping, a braided stream thick as my wrist splashing a dried puddle, refilling it to a bright red pool and creeping like lava beyond the puddle along a tire impression. Later it would clot and dry to a black mass.

"Let's get him dragged into the garage," Mr. Taggart urged us. He meant the open bay of the slaughterhouse with the steam boiler in the back, where we'd hung a differential pulley looped with heavy steel chain that was rated to lift a ton. We needed to raise the animal off the ground quickly so that it could bleed out before its blood congealed; there was a drain in the floor of the bay.

The steer had stopped kicking. We spread apart its hind legs. Mr. Taggart cut through the skin behind the Achilles tendons. We brought a wooden singletree fitted with meat hooks and set the hooks across the thick tendons. With Mr. Taggart's help, hauling on the singletree, we dragged the eight hundred pounds of dead weight across the yard and slid it across the concrete floor of the bay to the differential pulley. We spun chain to lower the big forged-steel pulley hook within range, fitted it through the eye of the singletree and then laboriously, putting our backs into it, clicked down the chain link by hard link to raise up the heavy steer.

Before we could gut the animal we had to skin it. Mr.

Taggart left us to our work. We started on its legs, cutting carefully behind the dew claws to avoid the tendons that supported it in the air, cutting a line down the length of each leg, snicking the tip of the knife through the fatty layer below the hide and skinning it around. We skinned out the tail the same way.

We needed sharp knives to skin the belly, to slice through the tough hide without setting loose the guts. We incised a line carefully down the belly to the wound of the neck, undermined the cut edges for a grip on the two flaps and pulled them taut while we sliced them free, two of us working shoulder to shoulder within the armature of the great carcass hanging upside down before us, the flaps opening like the doors of an ark. The steer had been castrated by clamping and its bag sequestered only yellow fat. We had to skin out its penis and cut it away. It was long and narrow as a riding crop but slippery and limp. One of the first times I was assigned to the butchering crew, when the death smell of the steer carcass nauseated me so deeply that afterward I couldn't eat beef for weeks, when I was still horrified by the flaying and the gore, an older boy on the crew in a fit of sadistic glee whipped a steer's penis around my bare neck like a hot, slimy snake. I screamed, tearing it off, and ran away sobbing. Learning the craft eased my revulsion, learning to steel myself. I came to understand, as any soldier knows, that slaughtering is human work like any other. I could go from butchering a steer directly to dinner and eat beef. "The craziness of these activities," as Ernest Becker writes in *The Denial of Death*, "is exactly that of the human condition."

We skinned the sides, the brisket, the rounds. We skinned down the back, thick with fat that popped greasily as we pulled the hide away. We tied off the esophagus with binder twine and sawed off the head, dragging head and hide together out into the yard, skinning out the head, sawing the skull to remove the edible brains and cutting out the long, dark tongue. Back in the bay we lowered the white carcass, shorter now by a head, to bring the rear quarters within reach, cut the anus away from the pelvic canal and tied it. However convoluted their innards, mammals are tubes topologically; by tying the esophagus and the anus we had closed off the tube at both ends, confining the odorous waste.

We sawed through the pelvic bone, widening the spread of the rounds. Then one boy, the crew leader—I in my turn— opened the belly and the great tun of guts slumped free. The two younger boys on the crew caught the steaming mass in a wheelbarrow pushed under the severed neck, stumbling before the sudden jumbled arrival: brown guts slithering and coiled, royal purple liver, pinkish white rumen like a fat man's paunch. The liver went off to have the gargoyle of its dark green gall-bladder cut away; out came the kidneys monumental at their small scale as Henry Moores and the foamy pink lungs and the giant's-codpiece heart feathery inside with parachute valves.

We saved the heart, the liver, the kidneys, the tongue and the brain; the rest of the guts, the offal, the younger boys wheeled off down the lane to burn while the older boys hacksawed the great ladder of backbone from stern to stem to split the carcass into halves. After it had chilled out overnight—hanging in the open bay in the winter, racked in a walk-in cooler inside the slaughterhouse in the summer—we cut it into roasts and steaks on the same butcher-block tables where we'd cut up chickens and processed fruits and vegetables before. Meat cutting was an entirely different emotional experience from butchering, a cool, respectable craft. No smell of death hung over it; the carcass wasn't hot; the meat had congealed and the fat hardened, and with those metamorphoses the tumult that slaughtering started in our hearts damped away.

Burning the offal, when I was new to the butchering crew, resolved the tumult another way—by etherealizing it. Only now, thinking through that strange experience in order to explain it, have I understood its significance. And understanding, I'm stunned by the unconscious ingenuity of healing and the force of trauma in this case that drove it.

What we did—what *I* did—was wheel the barrow of offal down the lane to its far western end beside a green pasture, well away from any buildings, where an iron grating had been bolted to a poured concrete slab wide and functional as the floor of a freight elevator; dump the slithery pile onto the grating; walk back up the lane, hose out the wheelbarrow, collect a can of fuel and a pocketful of matches; walk back down the lane, splash the guts with fuel and set them burning.

We were supposed to use only kerosene for fuel, since it ignites slowly and therefore safely, but I used gasoline—a gallon or more of gasoline pale red with lead levered into a can from the farm pump—splashing it over the guts, stepping back, scratching a match on a rock or the sole of my work shoe, throwing it into the center of the mass of offal already volatile and shimmering. The gasoline ignited with a whump! a shock of heat that blasted me back, forced me to wince shut my eyes, singed my arms and eyebrows and hair.

We were supposed to start the guts burning and leave them and get on with the day, but I stayed staring to watch them, got more gasoline and whumped! them again. I fell into a trance of watching: the tubing of the steer's innards inflating; the great rumen expanding like an alien life-form, like a nuclear fireball, its dome as it blistered to transparency revealing its rugged, brainlike interior strewn with the stems of green grass the steer had pulled for an offering in the last minutes of its life.

Sometimes the suspense of swelling was too much and I would shake myself from my trance long enough to find a stick and poke the swollen guts to make them explode, the roaring gasoline fire hot on my face as an iron. As the guts collapsed their contents oozed through the grating to the hot slab below and hissed.

And only when all was gore and smoking char did I leave that place and go about my work.

Sometimes our souls reveal themselves to us through small oracular openings. In *The Inland Ground*, immediately after the list of activities that I quoted earlier in this chapter, I wrote that I had felt despair at Drumm, "despair of my past and despair of my future." Life at Drumm made that despair difficult to "sustain," I explained curiously, "because the land and the animals and the work always called me back to those things that must be done next, to those daily regularities that insist on the continuation and preservation of the world." I then illustrated those daily regularities with examples that seem to me now, after a long passage of years, rather less than gregarious: "Cows must be milked," I instanced, "and animals fed, and these are certainties on which even loneliness must found an alleviation."

Isn't my choice of words there at the end once again a little curious? Shouldn't loneliness *find* alleviation, not *found*—that is, invent—it? Why would I want to invent alleviation and sustain despair? Mysterious. Cows are milked to feed people, and people certainly count among animals to be fed, so my examples aren't entirely vacant of humankind. But I wouldn't call them overly friendly either. Milk evokes nurture, of which

217

Stages on Life's Way

both Stanley and I had been severely deprived. Feeding is a kind of nurture, but it does violence to that which it feeds on, especially if people behave like animals.

My unconscious early prose—it was largely unconscious in those days because I thought the only way I could write was to get drunk first—screens a predicament I struggled desperately to steady at Drumm and continue to work forty years later to resolve: how to calm and to rescue the lurching monster of overwhelming, intractable, involuntary rage that my mother's suicide, my father's neglect and my stepmother's violence installed in me. Turning anger inward creates depression; that was the despair I found it necessary to "sustain," fearing that if I allowed my enormous anger release I might murder someone. Identifying with the aggressor—dismembering and eating animals as I felt myself to be psychically dismembered and cannibalized—disguises terror; that was the alleviation I managed to "found." Both were neurotic substitutions and therefore exhausting, but both strapped me together during years when I felt that I must otherwise surely explode.

Farm life is, literally, brutal: concerned with brutes, with animals. The word *brutal* has come to connote dullness and stupidity, but in its Latin and Greek and Sanskrit antecedents the word evokes senses of heaviness, weightiness and strength. It's kin to *gravid* and *grief* and *guru*, to *brio* and *brigade*. "Brutal" farm life is the human condition stripped of ideology, the human condition nakedly biological, and while that bare state may be primitive, it shares with the rest of organic life a quality that ideology promises but has never reliably delivered: evident corporeality, evident continuity. The "daily regularities" I found at Drumm *insisted*—I insisted—on "the continuation and preservation of the world." For two years my stepmother had so cannibalized my identity, had come so close to murdering my soul, that it was problematic if I would survive. Now I had been transported to a world of fecundity where animals were born, plants grew, we nurtured them and harvested them, killed them and ate them, stored up food against the barren winter, and then spring followed with birth and planting again. Survival, even resurrection were implicit in those daily regularities and I welcomed them with all my heart.

But until now I didn't realize how precarious I felt them to be. When I looked up the words "continuation and preservation" in *The Inland Ground*, writing this chapter, I suddenly found myself singing a hymn I had sung in church choir during my Drumm years, one of a dozen songs that reemerge from memory from year to year like recurrent dreams. "Seedtime and harvest" was the snatch of verse I associated first with "continuation and preservation"—seedtime is continuation, harvest is preservation—then "and cold and heat, and summer and winter." "While the earth remaineth," I remembered that the verse begins. It's from Genesis, I realized, and by then my heart was pounding.

I looked up the verse. Yes. Good lord. It's God's promise to Noah after the Flood, the Flood to which I compared my stepmother earlier in this book when I wrote that her "violence, the barricade of horror she built across my life, drowned my memory of those years—a dead lake entombing a green valley." God promised Noah that *While the earth remaineth, seedtime and harvest, and cold and heat, and summer and winter, and day and night shall not cease.*

But now I notice something more, the previous verses in Genesis that aren't part of the hymn but that I would have known even at fourteen, at Drumm burning offal, because I had read at least the first several books of the Old Testament by then:

that to elicit God's promise of continuity, Noah offered burnt offerings "of every clean beast, and of every clean fowl," and the Lord smelled "a sweet savor" and said in his heart, "I will not again curse the ground any more for man's sake." That's what I was doing in a trance alone at the altar with my offerings of steer innards: taking out the rage that the slaughtering had triggered in me on a part of the animal that was already safely dead; building a fire large enough to warm me against the cold wind of horror I felt still blowing at my back; but also sending up a burnt offering to God asking Him not to curse the ground anymore, asking Him not to take the wide world away, praying to Him to continue and preserve my life.

4

DAD AND OUR STEPMOTHER came to see my brother and me on visiting Sunday, once a month, for the first two or three months after the court sent us to Drumm. The woman wanted vindication. Not knowing where Drumm's authority ended and hers began, we sat in the car, parked with the cars of other boys' relatives along the dormitory side of the oval drive, and suffered her promises and threats. She was trying to talk us into coming back. She promised us money. She threatened that we would never see Dad again. Dad sat there taking it, just as we did.

Mr. Nelson was keeping watch. One Sunday after visitation he called us into his office. He asked us if our father or stepmother had given us money. He didn't allow boys to keep gifts of money from relatives; he didn't want differences in privilege to emerge among us beyond the modest differences in the allowances Drumm provided that were scaled strictly according to school class. We were supposed to turn in gifts of money for deposit in the savings accounts that Drumm maintained in our names, where my 4-H and FFA project earnings would go. Apprehensive but relieved, we told him the whole story.

Mr. Nelson probably knew that barring our stepmother from

221

the premises would invite retaliation, that effectively he would be barring Dad as well. If a man didn't protect his children from abuse, why would he fight about seeing them once a month? He made a Solomonic decision. Dad wrote to ask him why. In his reply Mr. Nelson invoked the authority of the law:

> These boys were removed from your home by order of the Judge of the Juvenile Court, and Mrs. Rhodes was instructed by the Chief Probation Officer to stay away from them. This was deemed best for the boys. It was part of the agreement, and any change will have to be made by the Court.

I didn't see my father again until after I graduated from high school, six years later. Stan says Dad wrote us letters for a year or so. He'd retired from the railroad and he and our stepmother had bought a piece of land on a highway in central Missouri near the Lake of the Ozarks, where she was opening a tourist knickknack store. "He wanted us to come and live with him and Granny in the Ozarks and help them with their place," Stan told me in Idaho. "I always thought, fat chance of *that*."

I don't remember Dad's letters. I remember that I was disconsolate at first on visiting Sundays when other boys had visitors and Stanley and I did not. Then, and for many years afterward, I refused to acknowledge Dad's complicity in what had happened to us; to do so would have meant also to acknowledge that the hole in my childhood could never be filled. I see that now. I couldn't then. I craved a loving, protective father. Mr. Nelson was too stern and distant, Mr. Berkemeier friendly and kind but impartial. What I needed I simply made up. I cried the first month when Dad didn't come to see us. The next several months I was furious, but with our stepmother, not with Dad. I thought he would have visited us if she had let him, which was probably true. I didn't allow myself to acknowledge that he had made a choice.

I taught myself denial. I armored myself with contempt. With other boys no one visited I hung around on visiting Sunday sneering. Delinquents were rare at Drumm, but we all prided ourselves on being tough. We compared muscles and calluses; I remember more than one boy deliberately pounding the calluses on his hands with rocks to thicken them, and I and others enjoyed nauseating little boys new to the farm by running pins through our calluses—not that skewering them hurt. Our spare twelve-man football team played junior-varsity football with only a rare substitution; we called ourselves the sixty-minute men. Those of us whom no one visited extended that tough-guy tradition to our derelict families, sneering that we weren't babies and didn't need Mommy and Daddy coming out to wipe our butts.

When sneering wore thin I retreated into books, reading ferociously, as I always had, to shut out the pain, but as I entered into the life at Drumm I advanced more and more outward to activities. From activities I learned a range of useful skills, grew more confident, won recognition that served provisionally as a substitute for love. Besides farming and school there was Scouting; there was church; there were FFA and 4-H; there were sports for every season—baseball, football, basketball and track. We had our own FFA chapter and our own sports program. Most of our activities took us off the grounds to Independence, Kansas City and beyond.

In a scrapbook that the Berkemeiers kept of their years at Drumm I find that in 1951, when I was fourteen, I was a member of an FFA poultry-judging team that competed at the district level, one level up from chapter; I was a member of an FFA radio-skit team that won first place in the state; I presented a demonstration—an illustrated talk—on "Livestock Loss" that won a blue ribbon at the Pioneer Community Fair and a red ribbon at the County 4-H Fair; I showed a red-ribbon gilt (a yearling female pig, my project that year, a notch up in responsibility from potatoes) at the Pioneer Fair; and I lettered in baseball, basketball and track. That was a beginning-level performance by Drumm standards, as the cases of ribbons Stanley and I had framed for the schoolroom attested. By the time I graduated from Drumm I had worked my way to Eagle Scout with extra merit badges in exotic subjects like Sheep and Welding for which the Boy Scout department at Sears had to dig back into its prewar inventory to find badges; I'd won at the state level in FFA public speaking, meat judging, dairy-products judging and parliamentary procedure; I'd been elected president of our FFA chapter and our 4-H club; I'd worked as a church camp counselor and lifeguard and served as state prayer chairman of the Methodist Youth Fellowship. I was one step away from being licensed as a Local Preacher, a sort of apprentice minister, in the Methodist church, when I would have been authorized to perform weddings, for Christ's sake, and even, *in extremis*, to baptize.

I took all these activities seriously, often too seriously. From a condition of abandonment and semihomelessness I was working my way into the middle class, which I imagined to be a safe haven; activities gave me protective coloration while I discovered and mastered the rules. At one point in adolescence I *read*, as a textbook, Emily Post's book of etiquette. I tried to teach myself to dance from an Arthur Murray dance book I found in the school library, but the experts who wrote the book, like those who write computer documentation today, had neglected the obvious; they didn't explain how to proceed beyond the little patterns of shoeprints they reproduced that I clumped out, flush with embarrassment, alone in the privacy of the East Building music room.

Activities offered ritual authentication and the approbation of adults. They were also the only culture available to me in that place at that time; I searched them for structures that might explain my alienation and alleviate it.

My second year at Scout camp, for example, I was inducted into an ersatz Indian tribe, Mic-O-Say, unique to local Scouting. A 350-pound Kansas City Scouting executive named H. Roe Bartle, a man with a booming, resonant voice who was later a colorful mayor, headed the tribe, and the high point of our induction was encountering Chief Lone Bear ursine in fringed buckskin as we danced around the kerosene-boosted Mic-O-Say council fire.

Crucial to our induction was searching out a message from the spirit world to pack into the small medicine pouch we laced together of leather and plastic gimp during our twenty-four-hour ordeal of silence and fasting. After sitting cross-legged on a bluff above the Osage River staring into the setting sun with a coating of mud drawing taut the skin on our faces and our chests, after an evening of solemn lecturing, we gathered a blanket and our unsealed medicine pouches and followed an older tribesman out away from camp into an open woods. Our guide dropped us off one by one in the darkness with instructions to build ourselves a campfire and meditate. I built my fire—since the debacle in Swope Park, I'd learned how ("Clear the ground, an ax-space around," the *Boy Scout Manual* advised)—and settled down to wait for a sign.

Nothing came and nothing came and I was beginning to worry. I was new at this. What we put into our medicine pouches was supposed to be an inviolable secret; the devil on my sinister shoulder whispered that no one would know if I cheated. Jiminy Cricket rejected that unworthy thought on my behalf—my face was all nose already. Comin' in on a wing and a prayer. I tried harder to concentrate. It started to rain, heavy drops first that rattled the dry oak leaves an ax-space around me, then a steady drizzle. I draped my blanket over my head for a hood. Before long I heard leaves crashing and saw flashlight beams sweeping the woods; apparently some of my fellow inductees were aborting their mission and heading back to camp. We'd been instructed to use our flashlights only for emergencies and to stay out regardless. I didn't think drizzle qualified as an emergency.

The rain hissed at my fire. Its slight flames faltered. One by one the compass rose of sticks I'd arranged faded from orange to rose to black. One small ember glowed on, unquenchable. I realized that was the incoming round I'd been waiting for, my message from the spirit world, a spark that the rain couldn't douse. I took it for a miracle and felt myself flooding with euphoria. Ardently I pulled a fresh leaf off a sapling elm, used it as a spoon to retrieve the glowing ember, folded the ember in, stuffed the hot leaf packet into my medicine pouch, laced together the last edge in the dark by feel, tied it off and hung the warm pouch around my neck. I'd hardly finished when our Mic-O-Say leader called us through a megaphone to put out our fires and come on in. I broke camp happily. I had my spirit medicine, a burning center that held back the dark. Over it, when I finished my induction, I was allowed to lace a plastic eagle's claw for a guardian: Don't tread on me.

Around that time—eighth grade, ninth grade—I wrote a

226

science-fiction story. I read science fiction compulsively by then, averaging five or six novels or story collections a week, hardcover books now, another step forward in my progression from comics through pulps to serious reading. When I finished with the entire three-shelf collection in the branch library at my high school I started again at the beginning. Early Robert Heinlein was my favorite, the future-history sequence that began with *The Man Who Sold the Moon* and *The Green Hills of Earth*. I made up a tune to go with his *Green Hills* title poem and remember at least a snatch of it now—"Let us rest our eyes / On the fleecy skies / Of the cool green hills of earth," the verse went, something like that. Ye who are weary, come home. Isaac Asimov's Three Laws of Robotics—rules with which all robots were supposed to be programmed to protect us from their superior strength—fascinated me; they offered an elementary exercise in logic and in ethics, subjects we weren't taught in school:

1. A robot may not injure a human being or, through inaction, allow a human being to come to harm.
2. A robot must obey the orders given it by a human being, except where such orders would conflict with the First Law.
3. A robot must protect its own existence, as long as such protection does not conflict with the First or Second Law.

Since I sometimes thought of myself as a robot, and feared cold and mechanical people like my stepmother, the Nazis and the KGB, I wanted Asimov's Three Laws to work. With real robots they might. I tried to postulate exceptions. My friends and I debated them.

The story I wrote was mystical rather than realistic. I drafted it in pencil. I used little circles for periods and the dots of *i*'s in those days. The story was about what happens to the souls of the living after they die. It proposed that *heaven* was a word for a kind of glowing white cloud of spirits that all came together in perfect love out somewhere among the stars. All the sad, lonely children, all the sick old people, the young men and women killed in their prime; the animals too, the deer and dogs and cats and even the farm animals that we butchered to eat, would all wake up after death and find themselves part of this glowing cloud. They would still be themselves but they would be everyone else too. They would know each other's thoughts and all their thoughts would be pure love with the hatred and cruelty gone. There would be so much love that everyone would be happy. They would float there for a long time before they realized that the cloud they were part of was God.

I read the story over and over to make sure I had it right and then I copied it out in ink on three-ring school notebook paper. I thought a long time about a title for it. I wrote the title in the left margin of the white space at the top of the first page and outlined it with a scroll: one word: *God.*

I showed *God* to a classmate, who pronounced it beautiful; he said he wished life after death could be like that. I suppose we'd all prefer heaven without hell, before death or after. I got an envelope from my box of stationery, looked up the address of the editorial offices of *Astounding Science Fiction* in an old copy I'd kept, bought a three-cent stamp from Mr. Nelson, who dispensed stamps from his office in grave transactions one by one, and mailed the story away. A month later a business envelope arrived with *"Astounding Science Fiction"* printed in the corner. I carefully slit the opposite end of the envelope so that I wouldn't damage the logo. The magazine had returned my story with a pink rejection slip clipped to the top. It explained that the editors were sorry they couldn't respond to each submission personally and so on. There followed a list of reasons for rejection. Someone had checked "Too Vague."

I didn't think my story was too vague. I didn't see how it could be any more precise than it was. I was sorry the magazine hadn't bought it but everyone was impressed with the envelope and the rejection slip. Simply to have received a response won me a measure of local fame. A piece of my imagination, such as it was, had traveled to another universe—New York, New York—and beings there had examined it; in some subtle sense it had altered them, just as the books I found in the library, even the books I only skimmed, altered me. I'd made an impression, however vague. I took the lesson to heart.

Reading the New Testament along with all my science fiction, putting two and two together as I'd once in grade school put the coasts of Africa and South America together and noticed that they fit ("Coincidence," my teacher had scoffed; "the continents don't move"), it occurred to me that Jesus might have been a time-traveler. If He'd traveled back from the future skilled in modern medicine that would explain the miracles. I described my theory at church camp to a girl I liked. "But then He wouldn't have been the Son of God," she objected. He could have been God's Son, I countered, if God had chosen to send Him back from the future to show people what the world would become if they believed in Him, to show them what His medicine and science would become. Jesus would have to be a good and holy man to be chosen to be God's Son. He'd have to be an adventurer too, because even if He knew how to revive Himself from death, He'd still have to suffer those terrible hours on the Cross with nails in His hands and feet and the wound in His side burning with vinegar. "You're really a brain, Richard," the

229

girl complimented me warmly, but I was too shy to kiss her good night—I shook her hand instead. I wished I could live in that future time when the leaders of the world would choose who would be Jesus and travel back into the past and work His miracles. They might choose me.

Later in high school I was saved, born again. In the fall of my junior year I noticed a girl in one of my classes—a pretty girl with teased, glowing hair—carrying a Bible among her books. I asked her about it. She told me she was a Nazarene. I told her I read the Bible too. She asked me softly if I'd accepted Jesus Christ as my Lord and Savior. The question was embarrassing but I told her I thought so, I knew at least that I believed in Him.

We walked a few times between classes. I told her the story of my life so far. She told me about Youth for Christ, about its regular Saturday night rallies, about being saved. Eventually she asked me if I wanted to attend with her. I took her invitation for a sort of date and said I did, but I didn't have transportation. We'll pick you up, she volunteered her parents bravely— Drumm was twelve miles out from high school.

If you've seen Jimmy Swaggart preach you've seen a Youth for Christ rally, although none of the preachers I heard came close to Swaggart's raw Hitlerian power. The lights were bright in the hall when we arrived, crowds of scrubbed young people and country-voiced adults streamed through the aisles, the green satin robes of the choir shone beyond the pulpit. My Nazarene friend was lovely beside me; we shared a hymn book and knelt together to pray. The preacher said that Jesus Christ had broken the old law of an eye for an eye and a tooth for a tooth with the wonderful message that every one of us was loved. That was something I wanted to believe and I worked at believing it.

Please Jesus come to me now and help me with Your love, I prayed silently. *I'll give You my life in Your work if You will lead me.* The preacher was calling those who wanted to accept Jesus Christ as their Lord and Savior to come forward to the railing in front of the altar and they would be comforted. Since I didn't know the routine yet, I waited and watched. My friend gave me a smile of encouragement, excused herself, slipped past me and swayed down the aisle. I felt tears start in my eyes at the thought of being saved, of being swept up and held and protected, but the tears wouldn't fall. I had to nudge them. I thought of being hungry, I thought of being beaten and a few more tears crept from their corners. I located my friend at the railing, took a deep breath and headed down the aisle.

My friend looked up with a face of ecstasy. She found my hand briefly and squeezed it. A churchwoman on the other side of the railing encouraged me with a big smile. I couldn't cry any more but I knew the few tears I'd coaxed before still clung. The woman patted my cheek. I bent my head in prayer and thought again about being held and protected and felt dissolved again. The preacher was working his way down the line. He stopped in front of me. "Will you take Jesus Christ as your Lord and Savior forevermore?" he asked me. I said yes I would. "Then you are saved," the preacher said, "and will know eternal life." The words embarrassed me and I looked down again. "Bless you, my son," the preacher finished. He moved on. I didn't feel changed. I was still watching myself. I still felt anxious and unsure.

After the preacher had challenged each of the saved in turn, he sent us back to our pews. The organ played "Nearer, My God, to Thee." I knelt again at the railing with my friend to take Communion. The preacher passed us little cubes of stale white bread. But as I chewed the bread and it dissolved in my mouth there came a great sweetness. Once again, as I had at my Mic-O-Say campfire, I flooded with euphoria. The bread tasted sweeter than any bread I'd ever eaten. Jesus must have sent a miracle of sweetness, a miracle just for me. I *was* saved then, born again, love-bombed. *Sweet Jesus*, I chanted to myself, *sweet Jesus*. Take, eat, for this is My body. I looked up at the painting of Jesus on the wall behind the choir and saw the tender look in Jesus' eyes and His hands turned out to hold me and I knew that He would always be with me and at last I was safe.

My euphoria lasted through Tuesday. I saw that there was a reason why the Youth for Christ rallied once a week; salvation had a short half-life. Saturday the Nazarenes picked me up again and we repaired the damage at another rally. It wasn't cynicism that corroded my conviction. I'd hardly discovered the uses of cynicism yet. It was rather that by then, at sixteen, I'd discovered how effectively and pleasurably masturbation at least temporarily relieved anxiety, and one act of such diabolic impurity immediately unraveled all my good intentions, especially since I found it difficult to leave my Nazarene friend out of the imaginary proceedings. So it was salvation and masturbation, masturbation and salvation until eventually my friend stopped calling. I think her parents got tired of driving all the way out to Drumm.

I was shoveling silage in those days at Drumm, shoveling silage and shoveling shit. We made silage in the late summer, feeding bundles of grain sorghum, which looked like emaciated green cornstalks with plumes of red-brown seeds at the top, through a violent, banshee chopper that slashed them into swarms of one-inch pieces, sweet sticky juice flying everywhere, and blew them fifty feet up a galvanized pipe into the silo. From bottom to top we filled two silos with the chop we made, tons of it, boys outside off-loading bundles of sorghum onto the rusty iron conveyer belt of the silage cutter, boys inside swinging the galvanized delivery pipe to guide the placement of the chop and marching around in circles in their galoshes in the humid late-summer heat juicily packing it down. It fermented through the fall and early winter to a heady, winy feed that the cattle loved. When frost killed their pasture we brought them into the dairy barn to the stalls beyond the milk cows. They slept in their stalls overnight. In the morning we pitchforked silage down to the base of the silo ladder, inside the barn, and fed them half a bushel each. As winter proceeded the silage fermented more and more acid. The acid rusted the steel bushel baskets that we used to haul it, steaming in the cold morning air. I carried two and sometimes three bushels at a time, for efficiency and for muscle building. The only way I could carry that many bushels was to bounce the stack against my thigh; by late winter the acid had eaten holes in my jeans where the baskets bounced and corroded my skin with itchy red patches of rash. When the silage got strong my city classmates slid away from me at their desks to give me room.

Shoveling shit was the alternative I'd chosen to milking cows. I had an aversion to milking cows. I don't remember now what excuse I gave Mr. Berkemeier for dodging that duty. I don't think I told him I didn't want the responsibility. I may have argued that my heavy schedule of activities made me an irregular candidate for a chore that demanded consistency. He understood, and I understood, that I was rejecting a position of authority within the informal hierarchy of older boys. I was, intentionally. I intended to make my mark beyond the boys' home. No candles under bushels for me. I convinced myself that milking was a dead end.

I volunteered to shovel shit instead, a chore most of the

boys despised. I liked it. Cowshit didn't smell bad once you adjusted to its intensity, not like hog or human manure. It smelled like vegetable fermentation, a farther range of silage. There were usually two or three of us on the shit-and-silage crew. I took a big steel scoop shovel first thing in the morning, after breakfast, worked my way down the stalls scraping mounds of sloppy cowshit and urine-soaked straw out from behind the cows, dodging an occasional hoof, then scooped my way along the concrete aisle gutters loading a deep, crusted wheelbarrow, wheeling the shit outside and dumping it into a holding pit from which we would later load it into a manure spreader and spread it over the pastures and fields. I worked up a sweat, I built endurance into my legs and back and arms, I studied the intricate mechanisms of leverage, I reveled in honest vulgarity, I challenged the institutional status quo and I finished half an hour before the milkers and won myself a few minutes more for reading. There wasn't time to shower before school, only time to change clothes. Between shit and silage it isn't surprising that our schoolmates gave us room.

But I don't believe social climbing, muscle building and a precocious relish for Chaucerian vulgarity fully explain my aversion to milking. Milk is mothering, milk is what our stepmother denied Stanley and me to drink, milk is the breast and nursing, from which at thirteen months I was probably torn away, milk is closeness and warmth and oceanic, unbounded beatitude. I tried milking only once. The cow's teats—like oversize fingers, dry and warm and leathery, like Dad's fingers when I held them as a little boy, like Dad's uncircumcised penis— disturbed me. The great bag of udder disturbed me with its mole-tunnel veins and its prairie of soft down, the gallons of warm, foamy milk it discharged, a Brobdingnagian breast. Milking I flew from. Shit I could face.

In these and other ways at Drumm I worked to construct scaffolding I could climb and foxholes I could hide in to escape the intense daily anxiety and the periodic visitations of horror that still shook me. The visitations were elaborations of flashbacks, as in posttraumatic stress disorder. They weren't confined to nightmares.

Unable to tear myself away from books, I was often the last one out of study hall at night. We were supposed to leave no later than half past eight so that we could be showered and in bed with lights out by nine. In the winter, when it was bitterly cold, I would stop compulsively halfway across the yard on my way to the East Building and look up at the stars. Out in the country the sky was black as a light trap and the stars were numerous, distant, high, white and cold. I never thought of them as warm suns diminished by distance. I thought of them as holes in the sky, stab wounds, diamonds that cut, alien intelligences. I thought they despised us and I hated them for it. We were pitiful and small and they laughed at us. They were utterly contemptuous; they cared nothing for anything on earth. *What,* I would always ask myself then, *if I were the last human being alive?* I would search my pockets for supplies to help me survive; I'd find a pencil stub, a rubber band, a folded note someone had passed me. I'd decide I ought to carry matches, and for a time I actually did: the vision was that real. *And what,* I'd ask myself next, *if all the buildings disappeared when the people disappeared, what if my clothes disappeared with them, what if I were left standing naked in a frozen, empty land from which all traces of human occupation had been removed?* I'd have to find a cave, I'd fantasize, have to wait for lightning to hit a tree and start a fire and make my bed in the meantime in a pile of leaves. That seemed improbable. Sometimes I'd fantasize that a girl would also be spared, that we'd find each other and keep each other warm and start a new race. Dark eroticism flickered in that fantasy. It seemed even more improbable.

It's winter in New England as I write. Walking back from Harvard Square to my house a few evenings ago in the cold, I realized what experience my fantasy of emptying out the world was built on. It was built on the winter weekends when our stepmother kicked Stanley and me out of the house in the morning and told us not to come home until night. When it snowed and I couldn't ride my bike I'd clump around all day from store to warm store, but when darkness fell and the stores closed there was no place to go, only cold doorways and streets cut with bitter wind. I'd pass houses where I could see families bathed in warm light gathered around supper tables. I'd stumble up the long hill toward the dress shop on East Ninth wondering if I would make it before I froze to death. That was when I first noticed how cold the stars were. The fantasy elaborates the association, connecting my stepmother's coldness with the stars, connecting the entire human world that allows children to suffer in the cold and the dark with the stars, annihilating it all. There are tens of thousands of such children as I was in the streets of American cities right now, and comfortable people prate about drug abuse.

Saturated with science fiction, I believed intermittently that I might be an alien. I happened upon a science-fiction story that reinforced my delusion. It was about a girl with a withered arm who is visited one day by grotesquely ugly aliens. They explain that they're cosmic tourists and she's one of them; her real parents were touring earth with her, disguised as humans, when she was an infant. They were killed in a car wreck. She survived with an injured arm and human parents adopted her. Now her people have returned for her. They take her to their spaceship, out in the country, and teach her how to change shape. She corrects her withered arm and then changes into her grotesque alien form. The story depended for its suspense on the outcome of her decision, to go with her people or to stay on earth with the adopted parents who love her. At the last moment, just after lift-off, the spaceship door opens and a dove flies out and you know she loves Earth too much to leave.

Sometimes I would lie awake at night silently calling to my people, the aliens I believed were out there who were supposed to come for me. I imagined that they could hear me. I believed I was withered too but the withering was inward. *Why won't you take me away?* I'd call. *Why won't you come and take me away? Don't you know I'm one of you? Let me fly with you, make me whole again, take me away, I'm yours, I'm not of these, I can't be of these.* But at that point I rewrote the ending of the story to reflect what had been and still was my despair, my fear that nowhere in the universe was there any possibility of understanding nor any margin of hope. I sensed my aliens becoming cold and indifferent, like the stars. Amused at my pretension, they laughed at me. I was sure I could hear them laughing. I understood that they would never come for me because I wasn't worthy of them.

Another science-fiction story probed farther into my wound. A galactic fighter pilot blacks out in the middle of a dogfight with an alien ship and wakes to find himself lying in a hot desert under a shimmering dome. A rock comes flying and hits him in the head. Dazed, he follows its trajectory back and sees that an alien has thrown it, the pilot he was dogfighting before he blacked out. The two civilizations, human and alien, have been long at war; a third, wiser and more powerful civilization has decided to resolve the war in a contest of single combat between these two representatives. The man soon learns that there's a force field between them; they can't attack each other directly, but everything else under the dome can pass freely back and forth.

The other creature is a gray, drum-shaped roller. It has a gash of a mouth and tentacles retracted into holes around its body that can lash out, roll it around, grasp objects and fling them. For a time it succeeds in weakening the man by the sheer volume of missiles it throws. But the gray roller is cruel, indifferent to the small creatures that live in the desert under the dome and pass back and forth through the force field. The man befriends the creatures the roller wounds, and eventually they help him prevail.

After I read that story I had a wrenching nightmare. I was the man, the gray roller was attacking me and no force field intervened to stop its terrifying advance. I woke shaken, soaked with cold sweat. The scene faded, but its aura of horror continued to unnerve me. I lay in the darkness trying to calm down. When I was calmer I closed my eyes to go back to sleep. Still awake with my eyes closed I saw the roller again. It was hanging on the periphery of my vision like a fogbank, waiting for me to fall asleep so that it could roll in and attack. If I opened my eyes it pulled back almost out of sight; if I closed them it rolled nearer. I fought sleep as I'd fought sleep when I'd needed to use the toilet at night during my stepmother years. Finally the roller faded and I slept. I suffered that hallucination more than once. It still makes me shudder. It was certainly a Sphinx figure, spiderlike, a *vagina dentata*, the gray fecal stick of death, a transformation into cylindrical form of the linear ledges of grasping claws in my recurrent childhood nightmare.

The sturdiest defense I build against these invasions in the middle years of adolescence I founded on two books and on a tradition I discovered within Methodism. The books, both of which consumed me, were Catherine Marshall's biography *A Man Called Peter* and Albert Schweitzer's autobiographical memoir *Out of My Life and Thought;* the tradition was John Wesley's unpretentious social activism, which made Methodism a liberal religion even in so conservative a place as Independence, Missouri.

Peter Marshall was a Scotsman who emigrated to the United States as a young man and entered the ministry, rising eventually to become chaplain of the United States Senate. He exemplified the Scottish tradition of muscular Christianity—rugged piety, manly faith, identification with Jesus not as the delicate, otherworldly neurasthenic of European Catholicism but as the robust young carpenter who made everyday life a sacrament. Muscular Christianity dovetailed sturdily with the tradition I found in Methodism.

Schweitzer was a more sophisticated permutation of Doctor Dolittle, sounding my African theme. He was an ordained minister and a controversial theological historian. In his book *The Quest of the Historical Jesus* he had argued that the real, historical Jesus could be separated out in the Gospels from the Jesus of conventional miracles and Greek metaphysics, who was a later interpolation (an argument which I took to be authoritative confirmation of the muscular Christian view). The historical Jesus believed that the end of the world was near (from Schweitzer I learned the word *eschatological,* "concerned with last things such as death, judgment, heaven and hell," a word rich with personal meaning that I larded into my writing for several decades thereafter). Since the world hadn't ended, Schweitzer argued, theology would have to come to grips with the fact that the Son of God had been fallible.

I understood a little of all that. I identified strongly with

Schweitzer's struggle to find meaning in the world. He'd been an academic dazzler, he'd been a concert organist, he'd helped restore some of the great organs of Europe (I read up on organ restoration and volunteered to help the organ builder restoring the organ at my church). But in the midst of his achievement Schweitzer had felt unfulfilled, and he'd turned to direct action. He'd gone back to school, become a physician, assembled a boatload of medical supplies and shipped out to the Belgian Congo as a missionary. Even in Africa, starting a hospital and tending the sick, he'd still been tormented—"exhausted and disheartened," he says in *Out of My Life and Thought*—by the dilemma of discovering some ethical basis for civilization, some elemental anchorage that might make ethics more real.

"While in this mental condition," Schweitzer begins the paragraph of his book that reports his revelation, "I had to undertake a longish journey on the river"—the Congo. He continues:

The only means of conveyance I could find was a small steamer, towing an overladen barge, which was on the point of starting. Except myself, there were only natives on board. . . . Since I had been in too much of a hurry to provide myself with enough food for the journey, they let me share the contents of their cooking pot. Slowly we crept upstream, laboriously feeling—it was the dry season—for the channels between the sandbanks. Lost in thought I sat on the deck of the barge, struggling to find the elementary and universal conception of the ethical which I had not discovered in any philosophy. Sheet after sheet I covered with disconnected sentences, merely to keep myself concentrated on the problem. Late on the third day, at the very moment when, at sunset, we were making our way through a herd of hippopotamuses, there flashed upon my mind, unforeseen and unsought, the phrase, "Reverence for Life." The iron door had yielded: the path in the thicket had become visible.

Reverence for life meant, Schweitzer explains, that a human being starts with consciousness, but not consciousness alone: the life that wills to live immediately finds itself in the midst of other lives that will to live, and they persist, he writes, "in spite of all negation of the world." And so "the man who has become a thinking being feels a compulsion to give to every will-to-live the same reverence for life that he gives to his own. . . . A man is ethical only when life, as such, is sacred to him, that of plants and animals as [much so as] that of his fellow men, and when he devotes himself helpfully to all life that is in need of help."

Jesus the time-traveler gone back to work scientific miracles; the girl with the withered arm who preferred the unsophisticated Earth that had been her childhood home; the pilot who defeated the gray roller by devoting himself helpfully to life; Jesus the robust carpenter; John Wesley riding circuit to spread the plain word of Methodism to the workingmen of England; the historical, eschatological Jesus approachably wrong about the approaching end of the world; and now Nobel laureate Albert Schweitzer finding alleviation of despair not in European sophistication but in Reverence for Life sprung up among cooking pots and hippos: all these eclectic discoveries encouraged me to believe that there was hope for me as well.*

I was piecing together a world. The farm was the ground of it, ancient and elemental under its multiple layers of allegory. It was sufficiently like a concentration camp to be familiar, but it was a concentration camp filled with food, a model for the real biological world. "The way of Providence," says Emerson, "is a little rude. The habit of snake and spider, the snap of the tiger and other leapers and bloody jumpers, the crackle of the bones of his prey in the coil of the anaconda—these are in

*They also systematically extract the pragmatic from the metaphysical. During my first year of college, a culmination of this trend, I abruptly gave up religion.

the system, and our habits are like theirs. You have just dined, and, however scrupulously the slaughter-house is concealed in the graceful distance of miles, there is complicity—expensive races—race living at the expense of race." The farm closed the graceful distance, and that was unsettling, but its plentitude ballasted me against the dark, recurring horror I experienced of the world emptying out.

These shards I collected, this bricolage, also share, at least implicitly, a solicitude for the small and the weak and the vulnerable. They encouraged me to believe that the child within me that I was trying to guard, the soul that my stepmother with my father's complicity had tried to murder, could be protected and nurtured. Two decades later, deep in therapy, I dreamed that an old garage was being bulldozed and a new foundation dug that would turn up the corpse of a baby in whose murder, years before, I was implicated. I felt horror in that dream at having done something irrevocable and an unbearable fear of being discovered. It seemed to me that no amount of wit or erudition or special pleading, no appeal to extenuating circumstances, could deflect the punishment that must inevitably follow. The dead baby was certainly the child I had been (or had not been allowed to be). I dreamed of it, writing this chapter, for the first time in years, and dreamed I shared its parentage with the woman I love. It was alive and well, bright and alert but small for its age, a little guy, chattering away at me, still in its crib, and I am past fifty.

STANLEY WENT HIS OWN WAY during the Drumm years. We were safe; he didn't have to take care of me anymore. That must have been a relief. We attended different schools at first and participated in different activities, and he was moved within a year or two of our arrival to the East Building to room with other boys his age, a move I felt keenly as a loss. We encountered each other every day, but we didn't spend time together. He kept his own counsel, even from me. I remember catching him once on his way into the East Building, blurting something about something I was reading—probably science fiction—and receiving in return an incomprehensible lecture about Plato's dialogues. He read Shakespeare for self-improvement, on his own. I hadn't found my way to the classics yet.

I remember one icy morning when the school bus started skidding down a long hill toward a dangerously busy intersection. The driver, a Drumm senior, had locked the brakes and didn't have the presence of mind to pump them. It looked as if we might skid into the intersection against the light. Fear froze us to our seats. Stanley, always fast on his feet, moved first: threw open the door, jumped out, raced down the hill ahead of the bus fearlessly into the intersection, stopped traffic waving his arms and motioned us through. I flushed with pride; when my brother caught up with us on the other side of the intersection and climbed back aboard, everyone cheered.

Stanley taught me to drive. I learned on a tractor first, a more forgiving machine than a car because the view is unobstructed in every direction, then in the carryall. With Mr. Nelson's permission Stanley would ride beside me after school two miles up Lee's Summit Road to the Twenty-third Street corner and back while I tried to coordinate clutching, shifting, accelerating and braking. He was a hard taskmaster, as he'd always been. If I made a mistake he corked me on the arm, jabbing my biceps with a sharp middle knuckle and raising a welt. It hurt. It made me flinch and distracted me from driving. My protests didn't interest Stanley, but logic did; when I finally convinced him his discipline was counterproductive he stopped.

I heard complaints against my brother, complaints about his hardness—he could be impatient of incompetence, as he'd demonstrated teaching me to drive—and defended him vehemently. He was rigorously honest and never to my knowledge deliberately cruel; if he was tough on others, he was tougher on himself.

He played marvelous football. He was growing up toward six feet, lean and lithe and quick. When he broke out carrying the ball no one could catch him. He was even more formidable at defense. Play after play he'd snake through the line the instant the ball was snapped and make the tackle. As a halfback he could position himself anywhere behind the line and he shifted from down to down. Coaches tore their hair. They'd double- and even triple-team him. At the last minute he'd switch to the other side of center, where the diversion of manpower made a gaping hole, and waltz right through. I remember hearing an opposing coach shouting at his quarterback once to stop that man from breaking through the line. "We can't find the guy, coach!" the quarterback shouted back in frustration. They called him the Ghost.

During his junior year in high school something happened that changed my brother's life. When I went out to Idaho I asked him to recall it for me. He nodded somberly. "That was a hard experience," he said. He hadn't told me before how he felt about it.

"We had Boy Scout meetings on Wednesday nights," he reminded me. "One of us would be the designated driver to drive the carryall. I was just beginning to be the designated driver, so I drove one night. The next day I was confronted with the fact that there were fifty or something extra miles on the odometer. That I had driven the carryall someplace besides Scout meeting."

"You were accused of having driven it?"

"I was accused of having driven it."

"Had you?" I'd never believed he had, but I'd never understood the accusation anyway and I wanted to be sure.

"No. Because I was in Scout meeting the whole time. There were several boys who ditched the meeting, and I figured one of them must have driven it. Gone to see a girlfriend or whatever."

Stanley didn't accuse anyone else of joyriding. Accusing other people wasn't his way. Inexplicably, Mr. Nelson didn't bother to confirm my brother's alibi with the Scoutmaster. Instead he announced that all the boys would assemble the following day in the schoolroom and vote—*vote*—on my brother's guilt or innocence. "Nelson washed his hands of it," Stan says. "He wanted the boys to decide."

"Why do you suppose he did that?" It didn't make sense.

"He liked me. He was unsure that I was guilty. He was afraid of making a bad choice. He didn't want it on his conscience. The closest I ever came to getting spanked or beaten by Mr. Nelson was when he grabbed me and shook me one time. But of all the boys he hit, he never hit me. I take that as a good sign. He had ample opportunity to. I remember when a bunch of us carried some hard-boiled eggs down into the cave"—an eroded hole in a pasture hillside, and wouldn't you think my brother might have lost his stomach for hard-boiled eggs?—"and got told on. He brought us into his office. I was sure he was going to knock my head up the side of the wall. But it was our first year there. I was still thin. So he said, 'Take this boy over to the kitchen and feed him eggs until he can't see straight.' I ate so many eggs that the poor cook took pity on me. 'Okay, that's enough,' she said, and I said, 'Thanks, I'm full.' "

We laughed at that, but I don't find Stan's explanation persuasive. I don't doubt that Mr. Nelson liked him. That only makes it harder to understand why he turned him over to the mob. My guess is that Mr. Nelson went public with his accusation before he had evidence or a confession to back it up and then decided to put the issue to a vote rather than admit that he'd make a mistake. He wasn't a craven man, but we all have lapses.

The public meeting was a popularity contest, and Stanley had enemies. I remember trying to lobby support, arguing the illogic of what Mr. Nelson had arranged. Some of my classmates agreed with me. A cabal of older boys who didn't like Stanley pushed for a conviction. They were gleeful. He'd stood apart from them and they were out to get him.

"It was humiliating," Stan remembers. A majority of boys

voted him guilty. He was grounded for three months. "I couldn't sing in the choir, I couldn't go to Boy Scout meetings, I couldn't do anything but chop wood."

"Weren't you just starting to date someone?"

"Yes," Stan acknowledges softly. It's too painful to talk about. "I was really very, very hurt. Nothing was ever said around me again about it. I just worked through my punishment. I didn't do it, but I had to go through it. I accepted that I had to go through it. And that was it."

"I remember losing touch with you after that."

"Yeah. I just really steeled myself up."

"And missing that. Realizing that you had withdrawn and that there was a door closed."

"I had to." Anguish in my beloved brother's voice. "I had to."

"I know you did."

"Otherwise it would have been unbearable. That saved me. Being hard to it."

"It was a very profound rejection," I sympathize.

"It was."

"From the group."

"And that's why I had to cut myself off from the group. That was some sort of turning point in my life, I think."

Stanley decided—"chopping wood," he says, "you know, and thinking deep thoughts and stuff like that"—to withdraw from the group that had rejected him. "I felt that the boys had been put into a position where they were acting on popularity. And it was obvious I wasn't popular with a lot of the boys. Trying to go around saying 'I didn't do it' to each boy was a waste of time. The thing for me to do was to concentrate on improving myself and to get out of there and to have something when I did. So I figured the best thing I could do was an individual effort."

He quit football and took up running, working his way quickly to five fast miles a night, around and around the residential oval at first and then, with Mr. Nelson's permission, off the grounds up to Twenty-third Street and back along the shoulder of the asphalt country road. "Getting out all the frustration by running was healthy for me and so I withdrew. I went into my shell. I was shocked and hurt."

"I remember you saying to me, 'From now on, I'll run against the clock instead of doing something where I have to rely on other people.' "

"I did everything within myself," my brother acknowledges. "It got so bad, Mr. Nelson pulled me in and said, 'I think you're hurting your body by running this way.' You know. 'I think you're overdoing it. Isn't this harming you?' I said, 'No, I love it. It feels good. I want to do it.' "

He trained through the winter and asked to run a high-school race that spring. "They put me in the cross-country. East High School had already picked their team, and Drumm wasn't invited, so they let me run unattached. Out of the entire city of Kansas City I came in third. There were maybe two hundred guys in the race. The East head coach was furious. 'Why wasn't this guy put on our team?' Because the best East did was something like seventeenth. So my senior year I made the East High track team."

That broke new ground at Drumm, since it took Stanley away for track practice and for meets at afternoon chore time. Mr. Nelson allowed it, how reluctantly I don't know. He may have felt guilty. He'd been reluctantly willing to allow me to go off for two weeks at a time during the summer to work at church

camps when the other boys were farming. Mr. Berkemeier may
have had a part in both decisions; when he became superintendent upon Mr. Nelson's retirement, after I graduated, he
opened the home up. Whoever decided, both decisions were
generous and fostering.

The summer between Stanley's junior and senior years
Drumm planned a camping trip to a state park in Minnesota.
My brother stayed behind. I wish I had. I'd have enjoyed the
time with him. Fishing, which is what the trip was about, bored
me. I spent the two weeks reading the Bible, the only book I'd
brought, and cleaning and frying up the hundreds of fish the
other boys hauled in.

"I said I didn't wish to go," Stan recalls. "I think Mr.
Nelson had a feel for what I was going through. He was not
unkindly, really, in his gruff way. He said, 'Well, if you stay
here, you're going to have to work. You're going to have to be
a hired hand and work.' I said, 'Fine, I'd be glad to do it.' So
Mr. Taggart and I worked together. He'd take pity on me every
once in a while and say, 'Hey, go take a rest.' He'd roll himself
a cigarette. He rolled his own. But I milked most of the cows
myself. I just went through them all. Milking twice a day. Did
all the chores I was supposed to do. Did the chicken chores. It
took me just about all day to do them."

In his senior year, 1954, Stanley managed a 4:20 mile, an
amazing time for a seventeen-year-old who'd only trained for a
year, close to the all-city record. That was the year Roger Bannister ran the first four-minute mile, a goal milers had been
attempting for twenty years without success, a magic barrier that
some coaches claimed would kill the man who achieved it. I
heard enough from Stanley about the four-minute mile to follow
the competition in the newspaper. Bannister was a loner, self-

trained, tall and lean and confident, an Oxford graduate medical student; I identified him with Stanley and thrilled to his upset victory.

Stanley had gone out to Los Angeles for a few days during the summer to visit our older brother and his wife. Mack had served in the navy, passed his high-school equivalency exam and become a motorcycle policeman; Angie was pregnant with their first child. They took him to Palm Springs. "It was beautiful in Palm Springs. I got a look at California and it was 'Don't look back.' My senior year I had a scholarship offer from the University of Missouri. Two scholarship offers, one in track and one in agriculture, because I'd won the individual 4-H national meat-judging award and was on the winning national FFA meat-judging team. I had another scholarship offer from the University of Kansas. And I don't know, looking back on it, I probably should have taken one of them. But I just wanted to get out of there. I'd already planned to go to California."

He graduated with a class of three other boys and left Drumm the next day. I remember how abrupt his departure felt. He'd arranged to drive two vacationing schoolteachers to California. I didn't realize until we talked in Idaho that he'd gone to the Lake of the Ozarks to visit Dad before he left for California.

"I went down there and stayed a couple of nights. I just wanted to see Dad and see how things were. Granny Annie went on this huge crying jag to me about how I had wronged her and I had told all these lies. She just cranked out the tears. I said one thing that didn't appeal to her and she immediately turned off the tap and started in on me like I was back there five years before. I just looked at her. I didn't say anything. I just wanted to get out of there. Dad was pitiful, basically. He had nothing left to say. It was like he'd been working for her all these years and he had nothing on his own to say to us at all, except 'Come on down and help us work.' "

Stanley went on to California to a difficult adulthood. Like me, he seems in some ways to be recovering from our childhood abuse only now, in his fifties.

He attended college part-time the first year after he graduated, when I was a senior in high school. He wrote me early in the fall; he was working as a janitor, I think, and paying his own way. When he'd arrived in Los Angeles, he wrote, he'd looked up the author of a book he'd read about space travel, the scientist Heinz Haber, and offered himself for training as an astronaut. Haber had informed him that he was too old; the astronauts, Haber said, were still in grade school. That was 1954 and Stanley was now eighteen. If anything, he'd been a little young. It's too bad Haber discouraged him.

For several months after that letter I had no contact with my brother of any kind nor any news. I missed him and sometimes wondered about his life, but I was busy that year myself. One night out of nowhere a nightmare saturated with fear and blood and desperation exploded my sleep. I dreamed that Stanley was in a violent fight, that his life was in danger. I dreamed his shadowy opponent smashed him in the eye—*my* eye. I felt the deep, sharp pain and saw flashes of light. It was the only time I ever woke screaming. I was living in a four-man room in the East Building by then. I screamed so loud I woke my roommates, none of whom were light sleepers.

Several weeks later Stanley wrote to tell me that he'd been in just such a fight. "That was the most horrible fight I ever had in my life," he recalled in Idaho. He'd been dating a Jamaican woman—she would become his first wife—and a previous boyfriend of hers, a black man, had attacked him. "The guy had on a huge diamond ring and he hit me right above the eye and just gashed me open. I had about thirteen stitches taken up in there." The blow caused a blood clot; for three days after the fight Stanley was blind in that eye.

As far as I could determine, Stanley's fight and my nightmare were simultaneous. I believed in psychic phenomena in those days. I'm thoroughly skeptical now. But my dream was probably psychic. Any number of people have had such dreams, and I don't know how else to explain the detail of the injured eye. My brother's fear and pain called out to me. I felt that close to him. Though we reside a continent apart and have lived these past thirty years in notably different circumstances, I still do.

CHAPTER

I'VE LEFT SO MUCH OUT. This is a book about the origin and evolution of the hole in my world, not a book about Drumm, but so much more happened at Drumm that I would like to tell.

I've left out the week in hot summer when Mr. Berkemeier assigned another boy and me to clean the flyspecks off the dairy barn windows. The windows were translucent brown inside with years of accumulated flyspecks, multitudes of black dots of fly waste resistant as hardened glue, as if some antic god had stripped all the periods from all the books ever written and flung them unaccountably against the interior of the Drumm dairy barn. Soaping clean those two long rows of six-paned windows in the summer heat, fraying durable rags rubbing my way down to clear glass to let in the day, I learned the blindness of con-viction: the fly legions had beaten against the windows because they were saturated with the small imprisoning light and couldn't envision the great light of the open doorway at the end of the barn that beckoned them.

I've left out my obsession with the mail. Mr. Nelson bor-rowed younger boys as runners to help him deliver the mail. When I was new to Drumm he sometimes picked me up at the noon hour, just before dinner, to ride with him down the long

front hill to the mailbox. He'd wait in his car between the stone
entrance gates while I ran to the country box on its post at the
side of the road and hauled out the bundle of mail. Driving back
to the West Building, steering with one hand, he'd sort the mail
in his lap and pass it along to me to give to Mrs. Scraggs to
distribute. On those expeditions I saw that mail, like books,
was a passageway to the outside world, a lode of secrets and a
semblance of connection. I wrote Robert Heinlein about a dis-
pute I was having with a classmate over a problem in celestial
mechanics and got back a cherished postcard confirming that I
was right; I wrote the author of a horse story about my life so
far and got back a warm letter from his widow saying how much
he would have appreciated hearing from me. I searched magazine advertisements for offers. There were fewer mail-order
catalogs available in those days, but they were free for the
asking. I asked. My allowance was only fifty cents a month,
cranking up slowly to three dollars a month when I was a senior
in high school, so I had to husband even the number of stamps
I bought. Within the limits of my means I ordered enough catalogs and premiums to provoke Mr. Nelson's tolerant complaint
at the volume of my mail. A catalog of magic tricks and party
items introduced me to the joys of the joy buzzer and the whoopie
cushion. I regularly received a newsletter from an organization
devoted to the invention of a perpetual-motion machine. I
couldn't afford to buy the wares in the catalogs I scrutinized,
but I imagined buying them, and in that way collected them
conceptually. Of all the free offers I solicited, the one I most
prized was a series of full-color posters of industrial operations—
a steel mill, an assembly line, a mine, a freighter, a refinery—
drawn in cutaway in minute detail. The posters exposed the
mechanical equivalents of the animal interiors I gutted; I studied

them obsessively for the same reason, to divine my fate. My study prepared me to write of more terrific machinery later, of nuclear weapons and the human heart.

I've left out hoeing corn. We did that when there was no other work to do, in the middle of the summer, weeded the field corn that would ripen heavy ears of flinty yellow kernels that we ground in the winter for animal feed. In midsummer the tall, tasseled stalks were spindled with dark green blades that formed a canopy over the space between the rows and shaded it; plunging into the corn was like plunging into a jungle. We started at the outside of a field, each boy taking two rows, the rows, contoured to follow the drainage, undulating a thousand yards along a section line. I hoed at a half-run with my head down, watching peripherally for the webs like fishnets that yellow-and-black field spiders strung between the rows to haul in prey, dodging around when I saw one to leave it to its work. My fine new hoe, oak-handled and square-cornered, the coat of copper paint on its blade hardly worn, was adept at weeds. It tripped tall ragweeds the way a running man would trip if you kicked his feet out from under him, the weed coming down with its severed butt and its leafy top hitting the ground at the same time. There's an art to everything or you make one, to amuse yourself, to look alive.

I've left out the arrival of television in the East Building living room: rushing over after class to allow the Army-McCarthy hearings to educate me to the credulities of my civics text; alone in the living room one Sunday afternoon with Mr. Nelson watching a live Hallmark Hall of Fame production of *Macbeth*, enthralled by the first theatrical performance I'd ever seen.

I've left out the calf I helped Mr. Taggart and Doc Tice pull. I was assigned to the horse barn that week, late in the winter, fourteen or fifteen years old, feeding the horses, cleaning out the horse stalls and sweeping the one-lane concrete aisle with a big push broom, easy work, work I enjoyed for the warm smell of the horses and the chance to practice skipping frozen horse turds down the long aisle and out the far door exactly as I skipped stones across the farm pond. We confined cows with calving problems in pens along the aisle opposite the horses. That day a little dairy heifer was trying to calve. The shorthorn bull had bred the heifer too young and her calf was too big to deliver. A rope halter tied to one of the pen's rough oak four-by-four bars restrained her. I stood at her head soothing her while Mr. Taggart ran his arm up into her womb to help the calf out. The cow was moaning and sucking in her belly. I wanted to cry for her. After he'd struggled for ten or fifteen minutes Mr. Taggart gave up. "You stay with the heifer, Richard," he told me. "I'm going to call Doc Tice." The poor animal was in agony; I was afraid she would die on me. Finally Mr. Taggart came back with the veterinarian, a lean, white-haired older man. Doc Tice set down his black leather bag and looked the heifer over. "She's in bad shape, Glenn," he told Mr. Taggart somberly. "Let's see what's going on." He soaped his arm and slipped it up into the animal's womb and felt the calf. He tried pulling it, his face reddening and sweat breaking out on his forehead even in the winter cold. After a while he said "Shit!" and extracted his arm. No adult had ever sworn in my presence at Drumm before. I was glad to hear his honest anger. "We'll have to cut it out of there," he told Mr. Taggart in disgust. They had to save the cow, but both men were angry that they'd lose the calf. Doc Tice found a wire saw in his bag, a long, knob-ended stainless-steel wire grooved with spiral serrations. He carried one knob up into the womb, looped the wire around one of the calf's shoulders, carried the knob out and worked the two knobs back and forth to saw off the foreleg. He removed the bloody leg, threw it onto the bedding straw and repeated the mutilation on the other side. Then, pulling as hard as he could, knots of muscle standing up on his arms, the cow bellowing, he extracted the dead calf headfirst. Its tongue hung out. I had to load its severed legs and its poor broken body onto my wheelbarrow of sodden horse straw and wheel it away before the cow recovered enough to defend it. I wept for that calf, wept and kicked the barn post and cursed God.

I've left out falling in love. I fell in love with a girl I met at church camp. She was tall and gracile, with a lovely voice. She sang, like an angel, "You'll Never Walk Alone." She lived in a small town sixty miles east of Drumm. I saw her only once after camp but in the year after we met I wrote her four hundred letters, more than one a day. She wrote me three hundred in return before she began dating and let our correspondence lapse. She dreamed of joining Fred Waring's chorus. I think I learned to write during that year of innocent longing, writing her.

I've left out lying on my back in the hayloft full of sweet, fresh hay, watching motes of dust materialize in the yellow beams of sunlight that filtered into the barn through cracks in the shingles, hearing a new litter of kittens mewing in its nest below the stairs. I've left out the stray dog we adopted, a cinnamon cur so crazy to fetch that it would flip itself head over end in the air and land upright with the stick in its mouth, a dog with mad eyes that would chase and wrestle back to its tormentor a sixteen-pound lead shotput. I've left out befriending a bully who'd been picking on me by helping him with his arithmetic and winning him for a bodyguard. I've left out sitting on a porch stoop for an hour or more after supper with a cat on my lap, petting the purring cat and watching the sun go down. I've left out loading the great severed trunk of an ancient black walnut tree—a log twelve feet long and four feet in diameter that must have weighed at least a ton—onto the flatbed of the farm truck to deliver it to the sawmill to be sawn into boards for our wood-working. We set a ramp of boards against the truck, beside the stump where the log lay, called out the entire population of men and boys, looped the trunk with logging chains and rolled it up the ramp by main force like Lilliputians loading Gulliver. I've left so much out. Drumm was a world, monumental and mil-lennial. I've left out almost everything.

In October of my senior year I attended college night at my high school. The East High counselor, a tall, kind, gray-haired woman named Anna Stewart, had advised me to talk to the Yale representative. I'd told her I would, and I wanted to, but my heart pounded when I approached the room—why get my hopes up?—and I passed it by for the displays of local schools.

At five of nine, the end of the evening, leaving the building, I passed Miss Stewart outside on the front stairway. "Did you talk to the Yale representative?" she called after me.

"No," I answered her, "I didn't see the point."

"Turn around and go back up there and talk to the Yale representative," she ordered me.

She would bear the responsibility. I turned around. The Yale representative was a young lawyer. He seemed to have been expecting me. He told me about a local Yale scholarship program, the Victor Wilson Scholarship, that was limited to residents of Kansas City, Missouri, and awarded on the basis of need rather than academic standing. He thought I might qualify. I had to pass an interview with a local alumni committee and I had to get myself admitted.

I didn't bother applying to any other school. By my senior year I had earned and saved a total of $250. I was offered a scholarship to a local religious college, but I was supposed to make an early commitment in exchange, and with Yale as a possibility I turned it down. I put all my eggs in one basket. That wasn't rational, but neither was my situation. A *deus ex machina* had been lowered onto the stage. Some higher power had heard and acted upon my secret wish, reaching down into my world possibly to lift me away. My first Christmas at Drumm we'd been invited on Christmas Eve to the mansion of a wealthy widower, Blevins Davis, who owned the show farm across the road, for refreshments and small gifts and the honor of admiring his professionally decorated tree. I'd heard that Davis was a Broadway theatrical angel. I wasn't sure what that meant, but I knew at least where Broadway was, and I'd fantasized hiding behind Davis's living-room couch when everyone else left, emerging on Christmas morning and offering myself for adoption. Now it seemed that my fantasy might come true in the corporate person of the Victor Wilson Scholarship. The Yale men who interviewed me could have been the alien uncles I'd been expecting. I couldn't bear to think that I might not win what I'd wished for so desperately. I was gambling, all or nothing at all, and any serious gambler will tell you that you don't bet against yourself. Applying to other schools would have jinxed me. It would have spoiled my luck.

I was primed to look east. Roaming the library, I'd discovered *The New Yorker* in the current-periodicals rack and scanned it every week. Its articles and especially its cartoons I found incomprehensible, not understanding the references, but I was skilled at fleshing out advertisements, and the world I glimpsed through the windows of *The New Yorker*'s advertising astonished me. I stumbled across an article in *Holiday* about the Ivy League that made the old universities of the East sound like the last bastions of civilization. Most influentially, if I went east I saw that I'd follow in the footsteps of a former Drumm housefather I'd idolized. Van, which is all of his name I remember, had worked at Drumm one summer, the summer just past, I think, after Stanley graduated. He was handsome and athletic and on his way to Harvard Medical School. I fitted him with Stanley's imago and followed him around like a dog. We talked about religion; we talked about philosophy; he counseled me; he treated me as an equal and a friend. Before he left I embarrassed him by begging him to take me along. Now it might be possible for me to move east on my own.

When Miss Stewart and I looked at admission requirements we discovered I didn't even qualify. I was short in math and science and had no second language. Miss Stewart conferred with the Yale men and worked out a remedial assault on my ignorance. Miss Vee Flinn, a rangy, eccentric spinster with a kind heart who taught math brilliantly, agreed to give up half her lunch hour to tutor me in geometry and second-year algebra. Yale agreed to waive its language requirement and to count my vocational agriculture courses as science. I signed up for the College Board physics exam. The alumni committee accepted my Aunt Pat's address within the Kansas City city limits as my legal residence for Victor Wilson qualification, reasoning that I was away at Drumm just as some of my potential future classmates were away at prep school.

Mr. Nelson allowed me to stay up after Drumm's cast-iron nine o'clock bedtime to study for the College Boards. To do so I needed a study area; the East Building housemother found a narrow room backstairs on the second floor that must have been a maid's quarters once. It was pure luxury, the first private room

of my life. I studied physics and reviewed English and history every night until eleven. I scored high on the College Board aptitude tests but below average on the achievement tests. "We knew you were bright," one of the Yale men told me later, "but we weren't sure you were literate." I'd never written an essay in my life. I hadn't read Jack London or Joyce Kilmer or Washington Irving. I still haven't. They should have asked me about Bruce Barton's *The Man Nobody Knows* or Schweitzer in Africa or *The Microbe Hunters* or *Madame Curie*. They should have asked me about the volumes of Dr. Eliot's Five-Foot Shelf that I'd browsed in the West Building living room; I could have copied out Elizabeth Barrett Browning's forty-third sonnet from the Portuguese from memory for them.

Whatever I knew or didn't know, I knew enough. Yale admitted me; the Victor Wilson awarded me full tuition, room, board, book, clothing, travel and incidental expenses for four years, a generous three thousand dollars a year. I stepped into the gilded car and it ascended from the stage.

The chairman of the Victor Wilson committee, a young investment banker named J. Willard Olander, whose family was in the livestock commission business (as Andrew Drumm had been) and who was operating a farm south of Kansas City in his spare time, hired me on for the summer. Jay and his wife, Martha Sue, made a home for me on their farm between my graduation from Drumm and my departure in September for New Haven. Jay needed a hired hand, but he also wanted to be sure I knew which fork to use. He sent me to his tailor. For four years he saw to it that my scholarship was renewed and cosigned loans to float me across the gaps between payments. The Olanders served as surrogate parents until I finished school. Later we lost touch. This is a good place to thank them, publicly, for all they did for me.

I began writing seriously in my early thirties. I'd tried before, but retreated into trance states at the typewriter that blocked feeling, so that the writing—a piece of a novel, a few short stories—emerged either mawkish or flat. I retreated in fear. I was afraid to speak out, afraid that what I had to say was worthless, afraid at the same time that releasing the rage I'd restrained across the years would be more than the world could bear. I'd had trouble eating since I'd left Drumm. Nausea welled up within me at the sight of food; at thirty-two years of age, five feet ten, I weighed only 132 pounds. A difficult marriage, depression, severe anxiety, heavy drinking to quell the anxiety, suicidal impulses, fortunately drove me into psychotherapy. Six months along in therapy, with a strong positive transference established and my anxiety somewhat allayed, I started eating and started writing.

I'd done book reviews by then, first for the *Kansas City Star* and then for the old *New York Herald Tribune Book Week* and *The New York Times Book Review*. Miniessays on the Middle West that I'd fitted into the interstices of some of my book reviews caught the attention of a *Book Week* editor, Richard Kluger, and when Kluger moved to Atheneum to publish books he offered me a contract for a book about the Middle West. Gambling again, I accepted. My first book, *The Inland Ground*, would be a montage: independent chapters, each on a different subject, that taken together might reveal the Middle West more concretely than one long narrative of gassy generalities. I wrote a send-up chapter on culture in Kansas City and another on a foundation man who was revitalizing the city's medical and educational institutions. Both chapters felt flat.

Then a friend of mine suggested I go with him to north central Kansas to follow a coyote hunt. We bounced across wheat fields in pickup trucks with wheat farmers who occupied their

idle winters coursing coyotes for sport. Their greyhounds and
Russian wolfhounds bayed from boxes built onto the truck beds
like camper shells; they dropped the dogs close in for the kill.
They didn't use guns. Their dogs tore the coyotes apart. On the
way home from coyote hunting we stopped off in another part
of Kansas to watch an evening of illegal cockfights. Men, women
and children with fists crammed with gambling money screamed
from the bleachers while fighting birds down in the cockpit
caparisoned with bright plumes stabbed each other with three-
inch steel spurs. Back in Kansas City after those bloody wit-
nessings I reread Ernest Hemingway's *Death in the Afternoon*,
got thoroughly drunk and splashed some of my violence and my
horror of violence across the page. The result was a chapter I
called "Death All Day," the first fully open writing I ever managed. I knew what it was; my hands shook from more than
hangover when I read it. Kluger knew what it was and sent it
on to *Esquire*. Don Erickson was editor of *Esquire* then, a Kansas
City, Kansas, boy, like me. Don sent Art Kane out to photograph
the fighting cocks and published the piece with fanfare.

I felt as if I'd cleared a choked spring. I've written well
and badly in all the years since that first breakthrough, the water
has run muddy or clear, but the spring that began flowing early
in therapy has never since been blocked.

In seven years of psychotherapy with a good man trained
at Menninger's I worked through the worst of my disorder. In
the meantime I left the corporation where I'd been hiding out
and began writing for a living. After *The Inland Ground* I dis-
gorged *Assassin*, tried to sell it, found no takers for its grisly
realism and stored it away unpublished. I wrote a novel about
the pioneers of the Donner party, bound for California in 1846,
who were forced to eat their dead to survive Sierra Nevada

exposure, *The Ungodly;* a novel about a white hunter in East Africa who sacrifices his life to save the woman he loves, *The Last Safari;* a novel about a gynecological surgeon going through a violent divorce, *Holy Secrets;* a novel about an Apollo astronaut whose son is kidnapped and buried alive against the payment of a large ransom, *Sons of Earth.* All four novels were published to good reviews. I supported myself that decade writing magazine articles on everything from a psychic dog to controlled thermonuclear fusion. Then, across five hard, rewarding years, I researched and wrote *The Making of the Atomic Bomb.*

Each of my books felt different to write. Each is set in a different milieu and tells a different story, in a different voice, in a different prose style. Yet I see now that they're all repetitions. They all repeat the same story. Each focuses on one or several men of character who confront violence, resist it or endure it and discover beyond its inhumanity a narrow margin of hope. Repetition is the mute language of the abused child. I'm not surprised to find it expressed in the structure of my work at wavelengths too long to be articulated, like the resonances of a temple drum that aren't heard so much as felt in the heart's cavity.

My first wife and I had two children; my second wife helped me raise them. I loved my children and worked hard to make sure that their upbringing was different from mine emotionally as well as materially, but after they were grown and I gained greater perspective on them and on myself I saw that unconsciously I had identified with them and had deflected their childhood partly into repetition, the same repetition that shaped my books. I had cast Tim and Kate as Stanley and me and structured the story to make it come out right. It did, more or less. At least they weren't physically abused. I wouldn't presume to say if they're happy. They tell me they are, and certainly they like their work, one measure of happiness; Tim is an architect married to his childhood sweetheart, Susan, who's an electrical engineer; Kate is a molecular biologist.

But despite therapy and work and parenthood I still drank heavily, drank more than was good for me almost every day for thirty years. Many nights I needed to hear the click as much as Brick did in *Cat on a Hot Tin Roof*. The click delivered me from uncertainty out into the ultramundane, into a cold, glittering darkness where I saw the world contemptuously for what I thought it really was, a blasted place, a mire of beasts contending. After nuclear war, Charles de Gaulle said once, the belligerents "would have neither powers, nor laws, nor cities, nor cultures, nor cradles, nor tombs." That was how I saw the world when I was drunk.

Writing was morning work by then and sober. Writing was better than drinking, writing was reverence for life, and in time I learned to crowd the worst of the bitter drinking into all-night marathon binges and to confine those binges to repetitive intervals eight or ten days apart, the longest I believed I could survive without them. Because they seemed to cycle I thought they might be chemical, and perhaps some biochemical imbalance mediated them, but I don't doubt that they boiled up from what was left of my rage. Serial murderers kill to the same compulsive meter. In great excitement I'd stumble upstairs to my office in a spare bedroom prepared to write out whatever grandiose vision I'd generated that evening. I had the good sense to leave my serious work alone. I wrote a few poems in the course of those nights and a couple of bizarre essays. Most of the time I stared. No experience of my life was ever lonelier.

I was nearly fifty before I found reason to let that anger

go. One fine day I met a woman who needed me as much as I needed her. I realized one night a few weeks after I met her that I would lose her if I savaged her with the bitterness and contempt I spewed when I was binging. I stopped drinking then suddenly and entirely, with enthusiasm, all at once and on my own, gladly, after thirty years, and didn't and don't miss it in the least.

Ginger Untrif, the woman I met—my lover now and closest friend—was then the most recent of the human beings across my life whose generosity of spirit drew me away from stark isolation. She wasn't my Stanley this time, though perhaps I was hers. We understood early in our relationship that we each protected within ourselves a wounded child. We cherish those children; nurturing and healing them is the mutual work of love we've set ourselves.

After *The Making of the Atomic Bomb*, to clear my head, I stuck a notebook in my back pocket and worked outdoors from fall to early summer on a farm among the glorious prairie lands of central Missouri beside a big, solid farmer who reminded me of Stanley. I moved back East, wrote *Farm* from the stack of notebooks I'd accumulated and woke up one morning convinced that it was time at last to write this book—to tell my orphan's story, as all orphans do; to introduce you to my child. There was a child went forth. He'd hidden in the basement all those years. The war's over and my child has come up from the basement to blink in the sunlight. To play. I'm amazed and grateful that he never forgot how to play.

Late in the summer after my graduation from the Andrew Drumm Institute, Martha Sue Olander restored an old steamer trunk for me, renewing its tin exterior with a new coat of black lacquer,

varnishing its wooden skids, lining it with flowered wallpaper. I packed it with my two new handmade sport coats, my button-down shirts and gray flannel pants, my Bible and everything else in the world I owned. Jay and Martha Sue drove me to Union Station and saw me off to Chicago on the Super Chief. I changed trains in Chicago for New York. Dazed from sleeping in coach while the train rolled eastward overnight, I changed again in New York to a suburban train and arrived in New Haven midafternoon. I'd never been alone before so far from any home.

I collected my steamer trunk, dragged it outside and found a taxi. Timidly I told the cabbie that I wanted the Old Campus. Take me to your leader.

"Shuah," the cabbie said.

"You know where that is?" I asked him, incredulous.

He looked me over. Another wiseass kid. Where'd they stamp them out? He shrugged. "Only about a tausand times today."

Cambridge—St. Croix, 1989